You Can Trust the Old Testament!

Refuting the Critics

2nd Edition

by
Gerald Charles Tilley, PhD

You Can Trust the Old Testament!

Refuting the Critics

2nd Edition

California Biblical University Press
P.O. Box 973
Tustin, CA 92781

Copyright 2019, 2024
by
Gerald Charles Tilley

Table of Contents

Table of Contents (cont.)

INTRODUCTION

It is popularly believed and widely taught throughout the world that the Old Testament is not historically accurate but contains many errors, contradictions, and discrepancies. It is therefore not only rejected in its claims to be the Word of God,[1] but also assumed to be unreliable as well as irrelevant to real life. The Old Testament is frequently dismissed as mere myth and legend, or at best a record of the religious beliefs and experiences of one human culture.

Like much that is popularly believed, however, these assumptions regarding the Old Testament are completely false. When one reads the actual biblical text as written, in comparison with other Middle Eastern literature of the time, the Bible does not show any similarity to the myths and legends of those cultures with which the Hebrew people interacted.

When the Biblical narratives are compared with the known history of the ancient Middle East, it is seen that the Old Testament writings accurately relate and reflect these otherwise known facts. And when the critic's specific attacks on the Old Testament are carefully evaluated rather than merely assumed, those criticisms are generally found to be irrelevant or just plain false.

In other cases, it is found that no information exists to either confirm or refute a specific Old Testament narrative. When no information is available outside the Bible rather than declaring the Bible to be in error, the honest response would be for the skeptic to admit he doesn't have any additional information.

In addition, the facts are, that the continued findings from archaeological excavations have repeatedly proven the skeptics' arguments to be wrong. However, even when the skeptic's argument is disproven, the skeptic rarely admits their error. They usually ignore or deny the evidence or they just change the argument. Later on, when most people have forgotten that the issues or arguments were disproven, some skeptics, despite knowing the claims have been proven false, revive and reassert these old arguments.

My purpose in writing this publication is the same as in all my prior books; that is to make more widely known some of the vast information that validates and confirms the reliability of the Biblical scriptures and the truth of the Christian Faith.

The word "critic" is not in itself a negative word. It refers to one who evaluates, analyzes, and critiques information and evidence. This is a necessary and desirable process and practice. However, my usage of the term will be in regard to negative or destructive criticism. I use the term to describe an attitude and practice that presumes from the outset what ought to be evaluated in order to verify or disprove.

The perspective of these negative critics is that the Biblical writings must be proven to be of merely human origin and filled with contradictions, discrepancies, and other errors. Their methods and intentions are directly focused on that goal. I use the terms 'critic' and 'skeptic' interchangeably.

Robert Dick Wilson, scholar, and past professor of Semitic languages at Princeton Theological Seminary, insisted that textual and historical controversies regarding the Bible should be removed from the subjective personal opinions of scholars and replaced with clearly attested objective facts.[2] This has not generally occurred.

Wilson's research has shown that most of the skeptical critics' work, often called by them, "*the assured results of modern scholarship*" is the very opposite. He revealed an actual absence of scholarship and a strong presence of subjective bias among the skeptics. Establishing the foundation of objective facts for the study of the Old Testament is the objective of this publication as it was his.

The first essay is titled, "Is the Old Testament Historically Reliable?" This essay was first developed for presentation at an apologetics seminar for a church in Madrid, Spain during the spring of 2005. That was my first of many ministry trips to Western and Eastern Europe. The essay has been expanded and segments of it presented several times since then.

My purpose in this essay is two-fold. I seek to discredit arguments and theories that are intended to undermine confidence in the Old Testament. My other purpose is that of presenting evidence and reasoning that demonstrates the reliability of those scriptures.

Most books are written by one author at some point during his or her lifetime. There are also many books that have writings contributed by several authors usually writing during the same generation.

The Old Testament is unusual in that it was originally written over a period of about 1000 years by approximately thirty authors in two languages in many varying conditions and locations. These authors are from a wide variety of backgrounds and vocations. Yet, despite all these variables, there is a consistency in outlook, great harmony, and unity among these various writings. The Old Testament was written from about 1450 to 430 B.C. The book of Job is probably an exception to these dates, having been written perhaps as early as 2000 B.C.

The second essay, "The Archaeology of the Old Testament" is a recent one, written for a different situation and added to this publication to complement the "Historical Reliability of the Old Testament." Due to the separate origination of the two essays, there will be some duplication of information.

This second essay begins with an explanation of the origin of archaeology, statements regarding the value and limits of archaeology in relationship to the Old Testament. Then it focuses on specific archaeological discoveries that confirm the cultural and historical context of passages as well as the confirmation of many particular details of the Old Testament text. While archaeology cannot prove the divine origin of the Bible, its confirmation of ancient historical events, peoples and places supports that conclusion.

Abundant evidence supports the authenticity and accuracy of the Old Testament scriptures. However, most people, especially in recent centuries, have not believed and embraced those truths. The prophet Micah gave an excellent summary of the reason for this disbelief. *"But they do not know the thoughts of the Lord, and they do not understand His purpose."* (Micah 4:12).

An interesting Sidelight

Though archaeology is usually considered a modern method of research and discovery, it is actually much older than usually thought. The last king of Babylon, Nabonidus may have been the world's first archaeologist. He had *"ruined shrines and temples to be excavated, old inscriptions to be deciphered and translated."*[3]

His daughter, Bel-Shalti-Nannar shared her father's interests. Sir Charles Leonard *"Wooley discovered in an annex to the temple in Ur, where she had been priestess, a regular museum with objects which had been found in the southern states of Mesopotamia— probably the earliest museum in the world. She had actually carefully catalogued her collection piece by piece on a clay cylinder."*[4]

8

Part One

IS THE OLD TESTAMENT HISTORICALLY RELIABLE?

The Critics Create their Own Myths

Professor Robert Dick Wilson, referred to earlier, had mastered all the languages related to the Old Testament as well as many other ancient and modern languages. He stated that, *"I have come now to the conviction that no man knows enough to assail the truthfulness of the Old Testament. Whenever there is sufficient documentary evidence to make an investigation, the statements of the Bible in the original texts have stood the test."*[5]

Wilson is correct. When there is sufficient evidence, the Old Testament documents pass the test of authenticity and reliability. However, skeptics usually will ignore or deny evidence that does exist. It is only when there is a lack of outside information related to the specific Old Testament text that the critics seem to have a legitimate case. "Seem to' is the significant wording here. This is because, as mentioned in the Introduction, when there is no related outside information an honest critic would admit 'we don't know.'

Unfortunately, there is little verifiable information available on the origin and earliest history of humanity. Neither is there outside confirmation for much of the early history of humanity presented in the introductory chapters of the Old Testament. This absence of confirmation is partly due to the ancientness of the times and events being dealt with. It is also no doubt due to the loss of early information. We do not actually know how early humans may have begun to record information about their own lives or that of their ancestors.

In addition, much of the documentation of ancient times that may have existed is no longer available. The perishable kinds of writing materials used at various times, such as papyrus and parchment, has contributed to this loss of information.

There has also been the deliberate destruction of a culture's records and artifacts by recurring foreign invasions, resulting in the extensive loss of information.[6] In addition, there has been some in-country practices of destroying records related to prior knowledge, previous rulers, their accomplishments, as well as other information. Unfortunately, these realities have all limited the availability of information about the ancient past.

This does not mean that there is absolutely no information about human origins and ancient times. In addition to the first few chapters of Genesis, numerous other writings have been found that attempt to recount the origin of the universe and humanity. Some of these accounts even parallel the Genesis account in basic structure and sequence though they differ as to theological perspective and specific details.

There is a very significant contrast between these other accounts and the one in Genesis. With one or two known exceptions, these other accounts are all filled with wild exaggerations as well as mythological elements. These include polytheism with gods engaged in gross immorality and violence.

The discovery that most ancient cultures have some kind of account of origins could lead to at least two opposing conclusions. One conclusion could be that somehow origins were communicated to early humans. This would lead to the further conclusion that most accounts have been largely contaminated by human imagination and speculation over the hundreds of centuries since then. Unbelieving scholars choose instead to believe the various accounts are all mythological and despite the vast differences in the Genesis account, they link it along with the others as mythology.

However, dismissing the early chapters of Genesis as myth is misleading. Even when using 'myth' in the technical sense as a religious text intended to explain the origin of the universe, of humanity, a particular people, customs, institutions, etc., this is misleading. It is misleading because myth also is intended by such scholars to mean the information transmitted is non-historical and untrue.[7]

Merely asserting a document to be myth in order to dismiss it, is not reliable nor scholarly. As Old Testament scholar Clyde Francisco wrote, *"The presence of a myth however, must be determined by objective literary criteria. Such methodology will at once reveal that, in the sense in which a myth was employed in the ancient Near East, there is no such type in the Old Testament."*[8]

Judaism has historically taught that long ago God revealed the truths of origins to humanity. It further taught that the ancestors of the Jews have maintained and accurately transmitted that revelation from God to the present day through the early chapters of Genesis. The historic Christian faith has always been in agreement that Genesis accurately transmits that revelation.

The Jewish people call their sacred scriptures the Tanakh. The Tanakh was originally written mostly in Hebrew with a few chapters of Ezra and Daniel in Aramaic. These various books of the Hebrew or Jewish Scriptures are usually designated outside of Judaism as the Old Testament. That designation will

11

be used throughout this publication. The sequence and organization differ, but the content of the Jewish Tanakh and Protestant Old Testament is identical.

The last canonical Old Testament writings were added to the Jewish scriptures about 425 B.C. Josephus writing about 90 A.D. said that no one dared add to the scriptures since the reign of king Artaxerxes I (465-425 B.C.).[9]

As to how the Old Testament canon was formed, we have very little information. We know that the writings of Moses were considered authoritative from their origin. The Levites were given responsibility for them to keep the Law (the Pentateuch) beside the Ark of the Covenant in the Tabernacle of God (Deut. 31:24-26). The writings of the prophets seem to have been given the same authority as they were written. Daniel for example writing not long after Jeremiah, refers to Jeremiah's writings as scripture and the "word of the Lord." (Dan. 9:2).

Some critics mistakenly assume that having been written in Hebrew was the basis for inclusion in the Tanakh. However, Ecclesiasticus, Tobit and 1 Maccabees originally were written in Hebrew, but were never considered scripture by the Jews. All three were excluded from their Old Testament canon.[10]

Other critical attempts to explain how the canon came to be include that a writing claimed to be written by a prominent person of ancient times was included Examples of writings that were claimed to be written by prominent people of those times include 1,2 Samuel, Psalms, Proverbs, Ecclesiastes, and Daniel. Another suggestion is that writings that dealt with the history of the ancient past (Kings, Chronicles, Ruth), or of the restoration (Ezra, Nehemiah) were therefor included.[11] However, the authorship of some of the Old Testament is uncertain. There are also books claiming prominent authorship that are also excluded from the canon.[12]

There is, however, more reliable criteria for the formation of the canon. One criteria is that, the writings agreed with prior revelation. Other criteria would be that a writing gave evidence of Divine inspiration and authority, and that the writer had credentials that confirmed his being a spokesman for God. It is apparent from 2 Kings 22:8, 2 Kings 23:1-2 and Nehemiah 8, that the earlier Old Testament writings had been considered to be canonical and authoritative by the Jews prior to those references.

Chapter divisions of the Old Testament were adopted from the Latin Bible in the early thirteenth century A.D. Current verse divisions were not standardized until the Hebrew Bible was edited in the tenth century A.D. by Ben Asher, a prominent Jewish scholar. Since neither of these divisions are part of the original text, they are merely for convenience of reference; they are not inspired.

These divisions can be misleading because a verse change sometimes happens in the midst of a sentence and a chapter change in the midst of a situation or explanation. So, one must give more attention to the thread of thought or information than to the artificial man-made divisions.

Most people seem to be of the opinion that the Old Testament is not a reliable or trustworthy source of historical information. This perspective is taught in public universities and liberal religious schools, and usually promoted in the media. This rejection of its historical accuracy then frequently becomes a reason or excuse to ignore its moral, ethical, and spiritual teachings as well.

These opinions of the Old Testament being unreliable are, however, contrary to reality. We will discover that there is more than sufficient evidence to show that the Old Testament is historically reliable. So, an additional issue to be addressed is the reasons behind such general opinions regarding the Old Testament being unreliable.

These scriptures were written over a period of about 1000 years. This was between about 2400 and 3500 years ago. Many of these documents were copied by hand for over three thousand years. With all the potential for errors and alterations developing over three millennia, it is of concern whether we can know what these writings originally stated.

In addition, with all the extensive changes in cultures and written language, how can we know whether the text is authentic and reliable? Not only do the words and meanings of language change, but the text was originally comprised of consonants only. There were no vowels in Hebrew to show the pronunciation of the words.

Asking whether the text is authentic is asking, how do we know that the text we have is what was originally written? Asking how we can know that the text is reliable means we are asking how can we know that what is recorded is what really took place several millenniums ago?

In other words, do we have essentially, what the authors originally wrote? That is the first fundament consideration. The second is whether the information is also true; is this what really happened all those years ago? These are the two more precise questions to be answered when considering whether the Old Testament can be trusted.

As stated previously, some scholars would equate the Old Testament as merely a collection of legends, myths, fantasies, and non-historical traditions. They assume the Old Testament to be more like the

Bhagavad Gita,[13] Gnostic imaginations, the Book of Mormon, and other religious fiction, rather than actual depictions of ancient history. But is this the reality of what the available evidence indicates?

Many Biblical scholars would identify the Old Testament with these fictional and mythical writings without any consideration whether there might be actual knowledge that indicates otherwise. Literary scholar, C.S. Lewis wrote an essay titled "Modern Theology and Biblical Criticism." He was writing in regard to the Gospels, but his insight applies to Old Testament critics as well.

Lewis stated, *"First then, whatever these men may be as Biblical critics, I distrust them as critics. They seem to me to lack literary judgement, to be imperceptive about the very quality of the texts they are reading."*[14]

Lewis explains that to make the judgments they make about the kind of literature they are studying in the Bible requires an extensive background experience of all these other types of literature. Without this wide and deep experience of literature, they lack any basis of comparison of the Biblical writing with actual legends, myths, fairy tales, etc. In other word, these critics lack the requisite preparation necessary to make valid judgments as to the type of literature that comprises the biblical documents.

Lewis goes on to say that in contrast with the Biblical skeptics, *"I have been reading poems, romances, vision-literature, legends, myths all my life. I know what they are like. I know that not one of them is like this."*[15] Lewis had the background to discern the characteristics of these various types of literature and knew the Bible was unlike any of them. He not only read these genres of literature extensively, he taught them and wrote a few of his own.

It might also be asked, as some do, what difference it

makes whether these ancient documents are true or not? Some Biblical scholars tell us that what actually is important is, the moral and spiritual lessons we can draw from these writings, not whether they are accounts of genuine historical events. But such scholars are wrong and deceive their audiences.

Actually, it does matter very much whether these documents are reliable records of historical events or not. For one thing, the documents are presented as if they present actual historical people and events. That would be deception if the people and events were not factual. It matters because the Christian Faith is based upon the reality of certain historical events presented in both the Old and New Testaments. if these events did not occur, then Christianity would be mistaken and fraudulent.

On the other hand, if the events actually took place, then the Old Testament consists of unusually reliable accounts of the ancient past. The Biblical writers' avoidance of the mythology and false beliefs of other ancient writers, should cause one to wonder how these records evaded that general contamination.

Biblical and linguistic scholar Robert Dick Wilson pointed out that the Old Testament is the history of the preparation of the world for the Gospel.[16] That is a major reason for its significance. That is also a major reason for opposition to it. Were the Old Testament to be acknowledged as authentic and reliable the skeptics would be faced with the issue of their own accountability to God.

False motives for attacking the authenticity and reliability of the Old Testament include the desire to avoid accountability for one's life. Another flawed motive is the intent to elevate human reason as the final arbiter of truth. Often these two motives are related. There are those who desire to escape any evidence that they have moral responsibility for their actions. Others seek to make God over into their own image or to revise moral truth so that it is in complete agreement with their preferences.

This distorted trend in religion is to eliminate anything not completely understandable and acceptable to human reason. To make God fully comprehensible to human reason would demote him to our level. When this is done, as in liberalism and some of the other cults, it refashions God into our image. The result is a man-made false god, not the true majestic and awesome Creator presented in the Biblical scriptures.

Each of these erroneous ideas is the result of misguided human thinking. Such persons have assumed the truly supernatural does not exist, and that there are no absolute or irrevocable moral and spiritual truths. They also seem to assume that human desire can create or alter reality or truth according to our own preferences.

Jesus referred to Abraham as an actual person. He mentioned Moses, David, Solomon, and Jonah as real people and their writings as factual. He referred to events in the Old Testament as if they actually happened. We see that Jesus accepted the integrity of the Old Testament because in his teaching and preaching he referred to them as scripture (Matthew 21:42; 22:29; Mark 12:10; Luke 4:21; 24:27, 44; John 5:39; 7:38).

Some critics have sought to explain Jesus references by saying Jesus statements didn't mean he believed these were historical people and events. They assert that Jesus merely went along with conventional beliefs to advance his own purpose and commend his own teachings. That such views about Jesus are completely false should be obvious for various reasons. First of all, such a practice would have been contrary to his character. He would have been deceiving his hearers.

Then regarding several conventional beliefs Jesus stated; "*you have heard it said*" and then countered those traditional beliefs with, "*but I say unto you*" (Matt. 5:21-48). He was asserting his authority to be superior to conventional wisdom. He also attacked the Pharisees for their false ideas, legalism, pride, hypocrisy, and lack of compassion (Matt. 23:1-36; Luke 14:1-4). He criticized the lawyers for misleading the people (Luke 11:46-52) and the Sadducees for failing to grasp that the scriptures clearly taught that there are angels, miracles, and an afterlife (Matt. 22:29-32).

No, Jesus did not merely avail himself of conventional misguided beliefs to serve his purposes, but confronted genuine errors of belief, practice, and morality with the truth. He clearly believed what he stated and taught.

Jesus' credibility is crucial. If he were mistaken about the historical nature of the Old Testament and its personalities, then we would have no reliable foundation for the Christian Faith. As Steven Masood has written, Christians have always accepted the validity of the Old Testament on Jesus authority.[17]

Several decades ago, I visited a class on the Old Testament with a friend at the University of California, Berkeley. The religion professor ridiculed the reliability of the Old Testament passages that were being presented that day. The professor's presentation made it look like God was incompetent and ignorant according to the information in Genesis chapter eighteen. The professor interpreted the passage to make it seem like Abraham was teaching God.

There was absolutely no consideration presented as

18

to the original writer's actual intent in presenting the information in the passage. Neither was any evidence presented that would indicate whether the text was valid or invalid. Humorous sarcasm and ridicule toward God and the Bible were the focus of the class. Unfortunately, this is a common practice when a skeptic or atheist does not have any actual evidence or valid argument to present.

Getting students to laugh at the assumed ridiculousness of the Biblical narratives is inoculating them against its truth. These students mistakenly assume the professor's presentation has shown the passage to have been proven false or irrelevant. This tragic error in thinking is encouraged by such professors.

This is a frequent approach at secular and liberal religious educational institutions. They frequently use sarcasm, ridicule, and completely reject any consideration of the authenticity or validity of the Old Testament text. They approach the text with total skepticism because of their biased training and perspective. They do not even think that there might be a different explanation of the text and possibly be evidence that would support or verify the Old Testament scriptures.

The following story about Sherlock Holmes and his partner Watson is very relevant to negative Biblical criticism. Created by the author Conan Doyle, Sherlock Holmes is probably the most famous person who never lived. Holmes is presented as the ultimate detective. In this story, Holmes and Watson are said to be out camping.

One night lying in their sleeping bags looking up at the night sky, Sherlock asked Watson what being able to see the night sky and stars told him. Watson began to extoll the beauty and glory of creation and the power of the Creator. Watson then asked Holmes what seeking the stars and all told him. Holmes replied, "It tells me someone stole our tent."

The point is that often the evidence is so obvious, so close at hand and even right in front of us, that it goes unnoticed, gets overlooked or ignored. The habit of overlooking, ignoring, or denying the evidence is extremely common when it comes to consideration of the Bible. The evidence for the authenticity and reliability of the Old Testament is quite compelling and convincing if it isn't over looked because of one's biased assumptions.

An example of the results of skeptical criticism of the Old Testament is revealed in this quote from Bruce Metzger's "Introduction" to The Bible Through the Ages: "*By such methods several traditional opinions have been virtually overthrown; for example, the Pentateuch is no longer attributed to the personal authorship of Moses but ascribed to a much later period in the history of Israel (probably the ninth through the fifth century B.C.).*"[18]

That is at least 500 years after Moses' lifetime. One early argument against Moses' authorship was that Moses never existed. When that was refuted, the argument changed to the claim that writing did not exist in the middle of the second millennium B.C. When that was disproven, the argument changed to declared that the type of writing in the Pentateuch did not exist in Moses' time. Then the written Code of Hammurabi was found that predated Moses by about three hundred years.

We now know that writing predated Moses by at least 1500 years in Mesopotamia. This was proven by the archaeological discovery of the Mari Tablets found in Eastern Syria by the banks of the Euphrates River in 1933. Writing as early as 3400 B.C. has been

20

documented in the ancient city of Sumer.[19]

Some have said that alphabetic writing did not exist in Moses' day, so the Pentateuch had to have been written several hundred years after Moses. However, alphabetical writing came into existence some time prior to 1500 B.C. In its early stages alphabetical writing consisted only of consonants. Hebrew writing originally consisted of twenty-two consonants.

We now know in fact, there were five different types of writing in existence by Moses' time, including hieroglyphic, cuneiform and alphabetic.[20] The critics changed their argument again to stating that Moses' writings were just one of many legal codes, not unique nor from God.

There was no acknowledgement by these critics that they were proven wrong over and over. They merely kept continually changing their argument. This practice of continually changing the argument makes it obvious the issue is not about Moses or truth, but about rejecting an authoritative scripture. Opponents of the Bible are constantly looking for excuses to reject and deny its validity.

It is evident that at some later date an editor made a few minor changes such as modernizing place names, adding remarks about Moses and the postscript of his death.[21] This was probably done by Joshua, who knew Moses intimately and is the only person specifically said to have added anything to the "Book of the Law of God" (Joshua 24:26).[22] This is no way invalidates the evidence of Moses authorship of the Pentateuch itself.

Other arguments against Mosaic authorship have proven to be no more reliable then were these.[23] It was argued that Moses was not a writer but an active leader establishing religious institutions and procedures. However, everything we know about

Moses is derived from the scriptural writings. These inform us of his leadership and legislation, and of his writings.[24] There is no reason that he could not have been all three.

Moses had the educational preparation (Acts 2:10; 7:21); he had the necessary information; and he had the time needed to write. As John Raven mentioned, *"Moses forty years residence at the court of the most highly civilized nation of antiquity was an excellent equipment to become the great lawgiver of Israel."*[25] Forty years wandering in the Sinai gave him time to write.

Another argument against Moses being the writer of the Pentateuch was that this type of writing did not exist in Moses' time. Hammurabi's code destroyed that argument as well. Then the argument changed again. The failure of previous arguments led to the declaration that Moses' writings were not unique, nor from God. They were than asserted to be merely another example of a culture developing its own legal code.

Though there are similarities between various other legal codes and that of the Pentateuch, there are also very significant differences. Other legal writings were only concerned with secular matters. In contrast, Biblical law interrelates religion with secular matters indicating God is involved in it all.[26]

Another major difference in the Mosaic Law is that the law codes of other ancient cultures apply the laws differently depending upon one's social status. The pagan law codes definitely gave preferential treatment to the upper classes. The Bible in contrast asserts that the law is to be applied consistently to all persons regardless of position or status. There are also legal statues in Mosaic Law to provide for the care of the less fortunate in Hebrew society.[27]

It has been argued, even recently, that Moses' writings do not teach monotheism, which means that there is only one God. Reading the Pentateuch itself refutes that argument, from Genesis 1:1 through Deuteronomy.[28]

Polytheism, or the idea of multiple gods, was always presented in the Scriptures as a pagan heresy to be avoided. Despite this, the Hebrew people were constantly being drawn away from the original vision of one God by the idolatry of the neighboring nations. The prophets had to continually remind and warn the people and their kings of God's judgement for their idolatry.

As mentioned, when the critic's objections are refuted or resolved, they will normally shift the argument somewhat to avoid the evidence that disproved their previous argument. If that option is no longer feasible, they will deny the existence of the evidence that refutes their prior argument. If that is not feasible, they may also declare the evidence to be insufficient, irrelevant or look for a new argument. This practice continues unabated today and indicates that the underlying issue is not evidence of lack thereof. The real issue is an unwillingness among many scholars to follow the evidence when it leads to unacceptable conclusions.

An important evidence of the historical reliability of Genesis, Exodus and the rest of the Pentateuch is the obvious background of these writings. The early chapters of Genesis reflect a Babylonian influence which would fit the time and culture of Abraham. The later chapters of Genesis and the remainder of the Pentateuch reveal the influence of Egypt due to the Israelites having dwelt there for over 400 years.

Someone writing five to nine hundred years later, as the critics maintain would not have known nor reflected the evidence of early Babylonian and Egyptian influence. Jewish scribes attempting to create a false history of Israel centuries later would have reflected the language, writing style and impact of Assyria, the Neo-Babylonian, or Persian empires, rather than that of Egypt. Egypt's power and its major influence on the Old Testament, was long past by the time the critics want to date the Pentateuch.[29]

The influence and impact of Assyria, Babylon and Persia are in fact shown in the later writings of Kings and Chronicles and by some of the prophets such as Nahum, Ezra, Nehemiah, and Daniel. Such influence on those writings adds to the evidence that the Pentateuch was written much earlier.

There are specific examples in the writings of the Pentateuch that show it to have been written by someone heavily influenced by Egyptian culture. Moses' writing style is predominantly that of prose, with very little poetry. This was consistent with Egyptian writing style which seldom used poetry as well as being consistent with the Hebrews having lived for generations in Egypt.[30]

Mesopotamian and Canaanite literature, however, is almost exclusively poetic. [31] Someone writing after Israel had been in Canaan for several hundred years or more, would have been more influenced by writing norms prevalent at that time and those cultures. Thus, had the Pentateuch been written hundreds of years after Moses it would have been written largely in poetic style. Some of the later Hebrew writing, hundreds of years later do reflect the influence of Canaan, such as writings by David and Solomon.

Another such example of Egyptian influence which would not have been evident generations later is the author's obvious first-hand knowledge of the geography of Egypt and the Sinai. Jews writing generations after the Exodus would not have had that familiarity.

The use of Egyptian words (loanwords), are much more common in the Pentateuch than in other portions of the Old Testament and Egyptian names are frequent. For example, the names Moses, Hur, and Phinehas are each Egyptian. Canaan is compared to Egypt and references are worded as if the author and people have not yet been to Canaan.

Archaeologist and Egyptologist James Hoffmeier has compiled evidence which strongly supports the accuracy of many specific details of recorded events in the early Old Testament writings. These include the correct price of slaves in the early second millennium as 20 shekels (cf. Genesis 37:28). [32] The price for slaves rose shortly after this time. Hoffmeier also shows that the lack of mention of the Pharaoh's personal name in the Pentateuch was consistent with Egyptian practice of not mentioning the name of one's enemies. [33]

Even Moses request for a religious holiday (Exodus 5:1) has Egyptian sources attesting to this practice. [34] The conquests in Joshua 1-11 are written in the style used by Pharaohs (especially Thutmose III) to record their military campaign details. [35] Minor details such as these show the culturally appropriate information for the era in which it is said to have occurred.

Much of the Levitical material in the Pentateuch has obvious Egyptian parallels. Though some critics have rejected the existence of the tabernacle as later fiction, claiming it is too early for portable religious buildings, it clearly has parallels with known earlier Egyptian design and construction. [36] These kinds of details would have been unknown by someone unfamiliar with Egyptian practices such as someone writing many generations later.

We have seen that there are many Biblical parallels with earlier pagan systems and construction, particularly those of Egypt. God has given instructions that will be familiar and similar to what is already known to a people who had lived in Egypt. Yet God presents clear distinctions as to the meaning and purpose of such similar things.

It is also significant that these parallels would be unfamiliar and meaningless to a people having lived in different locales and at later times. As mentioned previously, these cultural factors reflect the early date of the Pentateuch and refute arguments that later authors invented these writings.[37]

These and many additional factors listed by Hoffmeier and others argue effectively for an early date for the writing of the Pentateuch. Critics are reluctant to admit the evidence as well as the conclusions that can reasonably be drawn from that evidence.

Critics have claimed that the presence of Aramaic words proves a document to have been written later. However, there are also Aramaic words in documents the critics admit were early. In addition, Laban is called an Aramean in Gen. 31:18. He would have spoken Aramaic.[38] Also, cities that David conquered such as Damascus spoke Aramean.

So, there was frequent recurring contact between Israel and Arameans. This would make it natural for there to be some Aramean influence in Hebrew writings. As Robert Dick Wilson stated, *"Sporadic cases of the use of Aramaic words would, therefore, prove nothing as to the date of a Hebrew document."*[39]

A few years ago, Josh McDowell was beginning a lecture on the "Historical Reliability of the Old Testament" at a secular University. There was a large crowd of students and some professors. As McDowell began, one professor interrupted him saying, *"Aw come on Josh, everyone knows the Old Testament is historically unreliable."*

This might have thrown some speakers off track but not Josh. Josh responded, *"Tell me professor, what criteria you use, to evaluate the authenticity and reliability of ancient documents?"* The professor of course had not expected this comeback and reluctantly had to admit he had no criteria for making such evaluations of ancient documents. Josh didn't let him off the hook.

At that admission, Josh declared, *"You mean to tell me you have no actual basis for evaluating ancient documents but merely assert the Bible is unreliable without even examining the evidence because that is what is acceptable, and you consider yourself a scholar? That is arrogant bias not scholarship."* Josh then listed the three criteria by which ancient documents are evaluated. The first test is the Bibliographic. The second test is Internal Confirmation. The third test is External Confirmation. Let us examine each of these three criteria in regard to the Old Testament.

Bibliographic Evaluation

Bibliographic evaluation consists of confirming how many copies we have of an ancient document and how close to the original writings these copies are. In addition, ancient translations, and citations of the text in other writings are consulted and compared. Then using the science of textual criticism, we compare these copies, quotations, and translations with each other, checking for variations, additions, omissions, and consistency. This methodology enables the obtaining of a highly reliable text for the vast majority of the document.

Former Princeton Scholar William Henry Green

commented on the closeness of manuscripts to the actual date of writing. He said, *"The Hebrew manuscripts cannot compare with those of the New Testament either in antiquity or number, but they have been written with greater care and exhibit fewer various readings."*[40]

Prior to discoveries beginning in 1890 there were only 731 published Hebrew manuscripts of the Old Testament.[41] This, number, however, was greater than that available for any of the other ancient writings. For example, there are only 643 manuscripts of Homer's Iliad written during the eighth century B.C. Thucydides, The Peloponnesian War written around 400 B.C. only exists in eight known manuscripts.

Other comparisons are: The History of Rome by Livy, written during the first century B.C. or slightly later, has only twenty manuscripts. Caesar's Gallic Wars, written 58-50 B.C. has only ten manuscripts.[42] In comparison with other ancient writings and prior to modern discoveries, the Old Testament text was quite well represented though the manuscripts were relatively recent. Modern discoveries of more ancient Old Testament manuscripts set it apart, as the best attested of all ancient documents.

Old Testament scholar Gleason Archer states on the basis of the number of manuscript copies and closeness to the original writings, *"It is safe to say that no documents of ancient times have ever had such a full and impressive witness to the text as is found in the books of the Bible. It is highly significant that these non-Biblical texts are so cheerfully accepted even though for example works of Tacitus, Lucretius, Catullus and Aristotle have fewer than five extent copies each, and largely bear much later dating – than many Biblical texts."*

Archer continued, *"It is difficult to avoid the*

conclusion that the objection as to the trustworthiness of the text [of the Bible] is hardly sincere, but rather it appears as special pleading on the basis of a hostile bias that is scarcely worthy of responsible scholarship."[43]

Archer has informed us that the manuscript witness for the authenticity of the Old Testament is far greater than that of ancient classical works that are unquestionably accepted as authentic. He also pointed out the known fact that these Biblical manuscripts are much closer to the original writing than the manuscripts of classical authors. Thus, if the critics were unbiased, they would accept the Biblical writings as more thoroughly and more reliably established than the classical writings.

Instead, we have an inconsistent approach of scholars to the various ancient texts. The mention of gods and the supernatural in ancient pagan writings is ignored, but the historical information presented is accepted as valid unless contradicted elsewhere. However, in regard to the Old Testament, the inclusion of references to God is used to justify rejection of the historical content of these writings!

In addition to Hebrew manuscripts of the Old Testament text, we have the Samaritan Pentateuch which became a separate line of transmission of that text approximately four centuries before Christ. There is also the Greek Translation from the Hebrew, begun about 250 B.C. and completed by 150 B.C. or earlier. This was made for the large Jewish population in Alexandria, Egypt who no longer spoke Hebrew. It is called the Septuagint, often abbreviated as LXX.

At some time shortly after the return from captivity, or during captivity in Babylon, the Jews in Israel began to speak Aramaic. Aramaic had become the common language in Palestine. The Targums were originally oral paraphrases and translations from the Hebrew into Aramaic. These translations became more literal once they began to be written. The Targums were completed by at least the first century A.D.[44] They are not always of value in determining the original text, but are of worth in determining the meaning assigned to the texts by Jewish teachers of that time.[45]

Until the mid-twentieth century, the oldest manuscripts of the complete Hebrew Old Testament were dated in the tenth and eleventh centuries A.D. These are known as the Aleppo Codex and the Leningrad Codex. The Leningrad Codex is dated 1010 A.D. The somewhat older Aleppo Codex is no longer complete. One fourth of it was destroyed by anti-Jewish riots and fires in Aleppo, Syria in December 1947.[46]

There are also many partial manuscripts of the Old Testament. The most important of these partial manuscripts contain the Former and Latter prophets. It was made in 895 A.D. This copy is dated about thirteen hundred years after the final Old Testament writings. This last writing was Malachi, which was written about 420 B.C. Two other major partial manuscripts are from the tenth century A.D.[47]

The oldest complete text was a little over fourteen hundred years after the final writings of the Jewish scriptures and another fourteen hundred years further removed from the writings of Moses. All those years the writings had been copied and recopied by hand. Critics argued that we had no certainty of the original text of these writings after such a long time.

We knew the Old Testament text was consistent and reliable from about 500 A.D. to the present because of the work of the Masoretic scribes. These scribes added vowels to the previously only consonantal text and were very scrupulous in transmitting the text accurately.

Believing they were handling the very word of God was strong motivation to be accurate. The text they transmitted is called the Masoretic text after these trained scribes who meticulously copied the text for about five hundred years to 1000 A.D.

These scribes developed methods to eliminate scribal errors of omission or addition such as counting the numbers of verses, words, and letters of each book. Among other methods to ensure accuracy, they determined the middle letter, word, and verse of the Pentateuch and of other books and of their entire scriptures as checks on completeness and accuracy.[48]

Though the quality of transmission of the Old Testament text prior to the Masoretic scribes was not as certain, the Talmud recorded rigid rules established earlier for copying the Pentateuch.[49] This indicates the serious attempt made by the earlier scribes to ensure accurate transmission of the text.

This lack of older manuscripts caused Scholars attempting to determine the text prior to the Masoretic scribes, to be dependent upon the older Greek, Aramaic, and Latin translations, as well as citations of scripture in other writings. So, the discovery of more ancient manuscripts was greatly needed and desired.

The lack of older manuscripts is not surprising, however. The materials written on were of very perishable nature. In addition, Israel was frequently under the rule of foreign powers, was invaded many times and several of her kings sought to eliminate the worship of Yahweh. After the death of Solomon about 931 B.C., ten tribes rebelled and the kingdom split into two.

After Israel was divided into two kingdoms, the

Northern Kingdom was defeated in 722 B.C. and large numbers of Israelites deported to Assyria. Later, Judah, the Southern Kingdom, was defeated by the Babylonians, the temple was destroyed and some of the people deported to Babylon. (587 or 586 B.C.). Manuscripts and other artifacts were bound to have been lost and destroyed during these times.

After a remnant returned to Palestine, they were soon subject to Persian rule, then Greek, Egyptian and then Syrian control again. One of the Syrian rulers, Antiochus IV (167-165 B.C.), sought, to forcibly Hellenize the Jews by destroying their culture including their religion. He sought to eliminate the scriptures and made Jewish worship illegal. One could be executed for possessing a copy of the scriptures.

This led to a successful Jewish revolt and temporary independence. In 138 B.C. Antiochus VI reinvaded, took Jerusalem and imposed heavy tribute. Israel became free again after his death in 134 B.C. until Rome took over seventy years later.

The Jewish revolt against Rome 68-70 A.D. resulted in the destruction of Jerusalem including the temple and the end of the sacrificial system of institutional Judaism. There is no way to determine manuscript losses that must have occurred through all these ordeals.

Finally, there was also the practice of ceremonial burial of manuscripts discovered to contain errors or those worn and no longer considered suitable for use in worship. So, older manuscripts were disposed of in favor of newer copies depriving us of older manuscripts. [50] The unsuitable manuscripts were collected in a storage room called a genizah prior to the burial process. It should be surprising that after all this, we possess any ancient Old Testament manuscripts at all!

So, prior to the more modern discoveries, which are to be presented next, ancient translations of the Old Testament were the oldest witnesses available to the original text. These were primarily the Septuagint (200 B.C.), the Aramaic Targums (written at least by the mid first century A.D.), the Syriac Peshitta (mid-second to early third centuries A.D.), the Old Latin (about 150 A.D.), and Latin Vulgate (completed by Jerome in 405 A.D.).[51]

The first of the more recent discoveries was made near the end of the nineteenth century, in an old synagogue in Cairo, Egypt. Approximately ten thousand fragments from worn Old Testament manuscripts were discovered in a storage room (genizah). This room had been walled off and apparently forgotten. The earliest of these fragments were a little prior to the work of the Masoretic scribes from the fifth to eighth centuries A.D.[52]

These fragments helped to substantiate the validity of the Masoretic text. Some of these fragments were prior to the standardization established by the Masoretic scribes and were four hundred years earlier than our previously oldest manuscripts. Very few of these fragments, however, were available for actual study because they were sold to collectors. One large collection has recently been donated to Cambridge University.

Then in 1902, W.L. Nash bought an Old Testament manuscript in Egypt. It was initially dated between 150 B.C. and 68 A.D. Albright assigned it to the middle of the second century B.C., which has since been confirmed as a reliable date.[53] This made it the oldest known witness to the Hebrew text to that time. It included a damaged copy of the Ten Commandments, part of Deuteronomy 5:6-21 and the Shema (Deut.

6:4ff).[54]

The Dead Sea Scrolls

Suddenly, those fragments became much less important. Beginning in 1947, a huge number of older manuscripts of the Old Testament began to turn up. These were dubbed the Dead Sea Scrolls because of their discovery in various caves near the Dead Sea. There were many Biblical scrolls as well as non-Biblical writings of the rigid Jewish sect that had produced these documents in Hebrew, Aramaic, and Greek. Eventually over two hundred manuscripts and fragments of the Old Testament were found.[55] Every book of the Old Testament is included in the manuscript finds except Esther.

It has been said of William Foxwell Albright, the American Dean of Biblical Archaeology that, *"He made the archaeology of Palestine into a science."* Albright declared, *"the Dead Sea Scrolls as the greatest manuscript discovery of modern times"* and he is correct.[56]

The Dead Sea is about twenty miles southwest of Jerusalem. It is 1,388 feet below sea (ocean) level which is the lowest land on the planet. The Dead Sea is a hypersaline lake, 45 miles long and 9 miles wide in the Jordon rift. Jordon is on the east side and Israel on the west. The cliffs on the west above the lake are where the scrolls were found.

The Qumran community which had made these copies of the Old Testament text was inhabited during the second and third centuries B.C. into the first century A.D. [57] These individuals, had apparently hidden the scrolls in the caves for safekeeping in advance of the oncoming Roman army during the last third of the first century (68 A.D.). On their way to Jerusalem, the Romans destroyed Qumran.

The exact identity of the members of the Qumran community is disputed, and remains uncertain. We do know however that they saw themselves as an eschatological community that hoped to fulfill prophecy in order to *"bring the Messiah, end the period of gentile domination and finally restore Israel to a place of glory."* [58]

Many of the Biblical documents that were found in these caves proved to have been copied from 250 to 125 B.C. Others were as recent as approximately 60-70 A.D. The oldest of these finds is over one thousand years earlier, than any of the extensive manuscripts previously known of the Old Testament. The extremely dry and hot climate near the Dead Sea and storage in jars in the caves had helped preserve the scrolls.

Skeptical critics were elated, confident that this would prove that the modern text of the Old Testament was seriously corrupted. They were expecting that their skeptical and cynical attitudes towards the Bible and Christianity would finally be proven once and for all. Some critics assumed the scrolls were from the Middle-Ages, rather than earlier. This assumption has been proven false.

All kinds of assumptions were being made and wild claims asserted, about these documents, and what they would prove. A French scholar, Andre Dupont-Sommer, not part of the scroll publication team, sought to link the Qumran documents as the source of Christian teaching and that the sect's writings about the Teacher of Righteousness as the template for the Jesus of the Biblical Gospels.[59]

British scholar, John Allegro, an atheist who was on the scroll publication team, made, even more fantastic claims. He suggested three times on BBC radio that *"the Teacher of Righteousness was a messianic figure who had been crucified."*[60] Allegro's angry team members in Jerusalem, made a very unusual move. They signed a letter to the London Times denouncing each of Allegro's imaginary speculations as completely unwarranted by the scrolls.[61]

Allegro had apparently expected that his reputation, position on the scroll publication team, and the usual reluctance of scholars to contradict a colleague would allow him to get away with these distortions of the facts.[62] His falsifications destroyed his career.

In The Scrolls From the Dead Sea, American critic Edmund Wilson, relying upon earlier skeptical expectations about the scrolls, wrote that the Qumran sect *"is perhaps, more than Bethlehem or Nazareth, the cradle of Christianity."* [63] This also was complete speculation which proved by the scrolls to be totally false.

Unfortunately, once such speculations have been published, they have a life of their own. Many people, only hearing or reading the unfounded speculations, will continue to be deceived, not knowing such fantasies have been disproven.

Finally, after long delays, the actual texts of these Old Testament manuscripts began to be translated and published. This resulted in very different conclusions than the skeptics and critics had expected.

An authority on the scrolls, Hershel Shanks wrote, *"It is clear that the scrolls have not fulfilled the extravagant expectations that their discovery first aroused. Dupont-Summer was wrong. Jesus is not in the scrolls. Nor is the uniqueness of Christianity in doubt."* [64] The actual result of the discovery and publication of the scrolls is that the credibility of the current Hebrew text of the Old Testament was greatly enhanced. This then added credibility regarding the translations from the Hebrew text.

Shanks, a theological liberal, also acknowledged that, *"Although the Biblical texts among the Dead Sea Scrolls are a thousand years older than the oldest extant Hebrew Bible, they indicate that, all in all, modern copies are amazingly accurate. There are relatively few discrepancies between the Qumran Biblical texts and later ones."* [65]

So, despite a thousand years of being hand copied, very few errors had crept into the text. This is amazing, and completely contrary to the expectations of critical scholars and other skeptics. You may wonder whether the presence of some errors in the text invalidates its reliability. Would our ability to accurately understand the document be affected? No, the errors of transmission in the Old Testament text are not of that extent nor frequency. The do not invalidate its reliability nor our ability to comprehend the text.

Old Testament specialist Gleason Archer informs us there is no reason for concern that the text is either unreliable or incomprehensible. *"Not at all, for there is a great difference between a document which was wrong at the start and a document which was right at the start but was miscopied... by a simple process of correction in the light of the context, he may easily arrive at the true sense intended by the writer. Only if the errors which have gotten into the copies are so serious as to pervert the sense altogether does the message fail in accurate communication."* [66]

Later Archer asks, *"Do we have any objective evidence that errors of transmission have not been permitted by God to corrupt and pervert his revelation? Yes, we have, for a careful study of the variants (different readings) of the various earliest manuscripts reveals that none of them affects a single doctrine of scripture. The system of spiritual truth contained in the standard Hebrew text of the Old Testament is not in the slightest altered or compromised by any of the variant readings in the Hebrew manuscripts of earlier date found in the Dead Sea caves or anywhere else."*[67]

Archer further informs us that his above statement is easily verified by consulting the register of Old Testament variants either in Rudolph Kittel's edition of the Hebrew Bible or the Biblia Hebraica Stuttgartensia. He concludes that the vast majority of the variants are so inconsequential as to have no affect at all on the meaning of the text.[68]

As mentioned, the Dead Sea Scrolls include complete manuscripts or fragments of all Old Testament books except Esther. A late second century B.C. fragment of Daniel is among them.[69] So is a fourth century B.C. fragment of Samuel. These were more than a thousand years older than most of our prior text. Thus, we were now able to compare the transmission of the text from one thousand years earlier with the more recent ones. This has given the basis for greater confidence in the authenticity and reliability of our present Old Testament text.

Perhaps you have wondered how the manuscripts can be dated when the documents do not state the date they were copied and modern dating methods were unknown in the ancient world. Changes, from one language to another is often a clue. Another clue is changes in vocabulary as well as changes in spelling. Hershel Shanks explains some other means of dating manuscripts:

"Characteristics of handwriting, like styles of pottery change and develop over time. Based on changes in the script – the shape and stance of the letters, their relationship to a line, the order and direction of the strokes, and other such clues – a relative chronology can be developed. That is, the expert paleographer can conclude that one particular handwriting

specimen is earlier or later than another." [70]

The technique of dating handwritten manuscripts by the characteristics of the writing which Shanks refers to is known as paleography. It is important to note that recently improved carbon-14 dating techniques have confirmed the age of these manuscripts as determined by paleography.[71]

In his <u>Secrets of the Dead Sea Scrolls</u>, Randall Price wrote that not every single word in the Biblical text has been preserved exactly as in the original writings, *"Yet we can say – and say with greater confidence than ever based on the witness of the scrolls – that our present text is accurate and reliable, and that nothing affecting the doctrine of the original has been compromised or changed in any way in the manuscript copies."*[72]

There are even some variations in the text of different copies of the Biblical documents found among these scrolls themselves. Old Testament scholar Bruce Waitke wrote, *"Actually the variety of text types attested in the Dead Sea Scrolls underscores that their relatively large consensus is due to their close genetic relation to the original, not to collusion."*[73]

Waitke is saying that the variations in the texts is so minor compared to the overall agreement between them, and that this agreement is not due to copyists getting together to decide on a textual reading, but is because these copies are so close to the date of the original writings.

Randall Price states that our English translations of the Old Testament have not been changed by the Dead Sea Scroll discoveries. This is because the older texts are generally *"so close to the Hebrew text behind the Masoretic Text that they lend support to rather than emend those versions ..."* [74]

Shanks, writing two years after Price, indicates there actually have been a few changes in modern English translations because of the scrolls. None of the corrections or other changes effects Biblical doctrine. One of the more significant changes is in Deuteronomy 32:8. This is probably a justifiable correction from "*sons of Israel*" to "*sons of God.*"

Shanks then goes on to make the alteration of that text an excuse to make the unwarranted liberal assumption that it suggests polytheism.[75] In actuality Biblical usage of the phrase 'sons of God' is known and consistent. The phrase always designates beings created and dependent upon God for their existence. Shanks assumption contradicts prior clear statements in the Pentateuch that there is only one God (Exodus 8:10; 9:14; Deuteronomy 4:35, 39).

Bruce Waitke cites Douglas Stuart stating that, *"It is fair to say that the verses, chapters and books of the Bible would read largely the same and would leave the same impression with the reader even if one adopted virtually every possible alternative reading to those now serving as the basis for current English translations."*[76] In other words the variant reading, the critics make so much over, are extremely insignificant with only a very few exceptions.

So, the Dead Sea Scrolls did not discredit the Old Testament text, as critics had hoped and assumed would occur. Instead, the scrolls have strongly confirmed the reliability of the text of which we already were in possession. Once again, the critics were proven wrong in their expectations, their entire perspective, and their skeptical claims about the Old Testament! Despite this confirmation of the authenticity and reliability of the Biblical text, most critics have not surrendered to reality.

A wonderful example of this confirmation of the Old

Testament text, we have from the Dead Sea Scrolls is the complete scroll of Isaiah. This was 95% exactly as what we have today. The other 5% was nearly all obvious slips of the pen as well as obsolete spelling and grammar.[77] There were only three words in nearly one hundred pages in English translation that were uncertain. There was no change or effect on any doctrine. This is a spectacular example of the preservation of the text despite over a thousand years of copying by hand!

In Isaiah chapter 53, the great prophetic chapter of the atoning death and resurrection of the Messiah, only one word of three Hebrew letters is uncertain. That uncertainty does not affect or alter the prophecy or meaning of the passage. Another Isaiah scroll found in the caves of the Dead Sea area consists of chapters 41-59.

Neil Lightfoot tells us that, *"Both of these Isaiah manuscripts demonstrate that the Masoretic type of text was in existence in pre-Christian times."* [78] He also informs us that there are some scrolls that have agreements with the Samaritan Pentateuch and/or the Septuagint rather than the Masoretic text.

Most of the differences in these texts are merely differences in translation like those between various English versions. A few indicate a different type of text being used. [79] Some of these variations reflect the particular emphasis of this Jewish sect. However, the vast majority of the Dead Sea manuscripts support the Masoretic text.[80]

This confirmed that there was no significant difference in over a thousand years of copying the text by hand. Even some non-believing scholars acknowledged this was a spectacular indication that today we have a valid copy of the original writings. The Jewish scribes and scholars were very aware they were copying the word of God. They were therefore extremely careful in their efforts not to alter, add or omit anything.

In addition, the non-Biblical Dead Sea scrolls have demonstrated the thoroughly Jewish background and origins for Christianity. These Jewish origins are reflected in both the culture and the theology of the Christian Faith. This contradicts the efforts of some scholars who have sought to link the sources and origins of the Christian Faith with the Greek mystery religions or other non-Jewish, pagan roots.

Our English Old Testament is translated from the Hebrew text. It is important to be aware that, many of our quotes and references to the Old Testament in the New Testament are from the Septuagint (Greek) translation. Also, New Testament writers often paraphrase an Old Testament reference rather than quoting it exactly. This has sometimes created the illusion of contradictions between the Old Testament and New Testament texts.[81]

Internal Confirmation

The second test of authenticity and reliability of the ancient text is that of Internal Confirmation. This deals with the issues of any contradictions within or among the various writings. It also deals with consideration of any known anachronisms. An anachronism is anything from later times that was unknown at the time of the alleged writing of the document. Were there words used in the documents (other than obvious updating for understanding) that were only known and used much later.

Also, there were words used that would not have been known and used at later dates. This would confirm an earlier date for the document. In addition, it must be determined whether the text is consistent with itself –

whether the text has or lacks coherence. This means, does the writing fit together so as to make a unified whole?

Critics have claimed that the Old Testament text violates each of these elements or criteria. However, as we carefully evaluate the specific charges against the Old Testament, the vast majority are easily dissolved. Even the more difficult critical attacks can be answered and resolved. The skeptics' criticisms are mostly cases of ignoring the literary, historical/cultural context of each writing or are arguments from silence. The Old Testament meets the internal tests wonderfully. There are no actual anachronisms, no contradictions of known history and an exceptional internal consistency throughout.

Conservative and objective scholars acknowledge that most problems and alleged contradictions in the Bible are cleared up by a careful study of the supposed difficulty within its literary and cultural contexts.

Arguments from silence means that whenever something mentioned in the Old Testament (a person, city, event, etc.) was unknown outside of the Biblical reference, the critics declared the Bible to be in error. They assumed and asserted that the information presented in the Bible was merely folklore, legend or mythological.

To make such declarations is basically a dishonest approach to the text. A lack of corroboration does not prove an error, but merely shows the critic has no external information upon which to make a valid decision regarding that particular passage or event. Arguments from silence will be dealt with more extensively under the heading of *External Evidence*.

Another approach of critics is to assert, without any evidence, that a statement in the Bible is an error because they disagree with the information. They then declare that this proves that the Bible is merely of human rather than divine origin. It is important to remember that declaring the Bible to be in error is not the same as proving the Bible guilty of error. Anything can be asserted, but to be valid an assertion must be verified by evidence.

Another method related to the one above is to make false claims as to what the Bible does or does not teach. The famous British philosopher Bertrand Russell was guilty of this. Russell stated that the question of usury or charging interest was not addressed in the Bible.

However, Exodus 22:25 declares that those lending money to the poor among them are not to charge interest. See Leviticus 25:35-37. Deuteronomy 23:19-20 states that foreigners can be charged interest but not their fellow Jews. Nehemiah 5:7-10 tells the nobles to stop the practice of usury and return the interest to their fellow Jews who have returned to Jerusalem from Babylon. Obviously, Russell was mistaken.

Each of the Old Testament writings show coherence when actually read as written. The entire Old Testament text shows a unity, harmony and coherence that is at least equal, if not superior, to that of other extensive ancient documents. The unity of the Old Testament is significant, with a remarkable singleness of purpose and theme despite all the variables of time, situation, variety of authors etc. which suggests strongly the operation of a single mind behind it all.[82]

The Old Testament is consistent from the first chapters of Genesis through Malachi in assuming and often directly asserting monotheism. It is also consistent in opposing the worship of any God but Yahweh, and the condemnation of worship of other gods as idolatry. The attributes of God are also consistent in portraying God as the infinite, all-powerful and sovereign Creator.

Early Skeptical Attacks On The Old Testament

These skeptical scholars, currently often called minimalists, are certain the Old Testament cannot have been revealed by God. As a result of their assumptions, they look for anything that can possibly suggest errors or discrepancies in the text and devise methods of attempting to discredit the scriptures in order to justify their rejection of those writings. That the Pentateuch was written by Moses was universally accepted by Jews and Christians until the late seventeenth century.

The Jewish philosopher Benedict Spinoza, a pantheist, declared in his <u>Tractatus Theologico-Politicus</u> (1670) that Abraham Ibn Ezra didn't believe Moses wrote the Pentateuch. Ezra had been a very significant and influential Jewish Rabbi and philosopher in the twelfth century. Quotations from Ibn Ezra however disproved Spinoza's claim about him. Spinoza didn't accept that Moses had written the Pentateuch and gave a few arguments in support of his disbelief.[83]

One of Spinoza's arguments was that Numbers 12:3 states that Moses was a most humble man, and that a humble man would not assert his humility. This is obviously a later comment added by Joshua or possibly Ezra. Another argument was that Moses was referred to in the Pentateuch in the third person which the author would not do. Actually, authors do that often instead of constantly referring to themselves in the first person.

Spinoza also said that Moses obviously did not write his own obituary. That is true, but author's obituaries were frequently added to the end of their writings in ancient times, especially if they had died shortly after completing the writings. [84] These objections were quite easily refuted. Such later editorial additions to the text do not invalidate Moses as the writer of the books. Despite being invalid, these same arguments are still used today.

Another apostate Jew, a French physician, Jean Austruc, took up the attack against Moses. Austruc's 1753 book, <u>Conjectures sur la Genese</u> suggested that the different names for God revealed that there were originally several separate documents that lay behind the present text that had been edited and combined.[85] These earlier arguments and attacks against Moses' authorship of the Pentateuch were thoroughly refuted back then. Though such arguments were complete speculation without any real basis, skeptics continue to revive them.

This skepticism has increased among secular and liberal scholars over the past several centuries. In 1895, the entire book of Genesis was declared by Hermann Gunkel to be legend, not history.[86] Some have even gone to the ridiculous extreme of dicing and splicing the early books of the Bible into various segments and dating them much later than they were written. These have been attempts to discredit the belief that the scriptures are from God, that Moses was the writer, and to destroy the evidence of the early teaching of monotheism.

Refuting The Documentary Hypothesis

The most widely known of these cut-and-paste jobs was by the German scholar, Julius Wellhausen, who published his <u>Prologue to the History of Israel</u> in 1878. Wellhausen's fantasy is known as the Documentary Hypothesis. He created a massive amount of detailed analysis to give these ideas the appearance of

46

credibility. He made declarations and claims as though there was obvious evidence to support his theory.

Though there was, and is, absolutely no evidence to support these conjectures, they were adopted as valid by unbelieving scholars of religion. This was partly due to the relatively new adoption of Darwin's theory of the evolution of the species. It is also due to the theory giving the illusion of scholarly reasons to rejects the Old Testament text.

In my previous books, I have written critiques showing the reasons that Wellhausen's theory should be jettisoned (*Defending the Christian Faith*, volume I and more briefly in *The Bible: An Introduction*). I will also include criticism of his imaginary reconstruction of the Pentateuch and distortion of the history of Israel in this volume.

I continue to attack Wellhausen's theory because despite the theory being totally contradicted by both known history, comparative religion, anthropology and archaeology, adaptations of the theory are still widely taught and promoted even in recent theological writings. The theory is held tenaciously because it seems to support the preferences of the theological world outside of Evangelicalism.

However, if someone takes the theory's assumptions one-by-one apart from a biased perspective, and evaluates that assumption in the light of known facts, the truth quickly becomes obvious that the Documentary Hypothesis is a collection of completely unsupportable speculations and assumptions.

As I have written previously, Wellhausen based his theory upon another theory published only a few years before his own. Edward B. Taylor had adopted and adapted the then recent theory of evolution to the origin of religion. Taylor's book Primitive Culture

(1871) assumed the process of development of religion from simple primitive beginnings, slowly advancing through animism and pantheism to polytheism, henotheism and eventually arriving at monotheism.

Anthropologist Andrew Lang, mentored by Taylor, was surprised to find that his research in anthropology completely refuted Taylor's theory. Lang's findings were ignored and rejected by other anthropologists at first. However, despite the initial ridicule and rejection of Lang's data, many other anthropologists began to discover that behind the mythology of the supposedly primitive tribes was an earlier concept of one supreme Deity.

Lang published his findings in 1898. Other anthropologists published confirming information from all over the world soon thereafter. However, neither Taylor nor Wellhausen were willing to allow the discovery of this information to influence their theories.

A major assumption by Wellhausen was that which Austruc had mentioned earlier. He assumed that each different name for God in the Pentateuch was evidence of a separate author. He cut up and spliced together the text of the Pentateuch based upon this and other unwarranted assumptions. He did this despite there being no manuscript or other evidence to support his theory.

Another major assumption was Wehausen's declaration that the Tabernacle never existed because such structures didn't exist until much later in history. The problem with this assertion is that portable structures like it have been found to have existed in Egypt as early as 2600 B.C.[87] That is more than a thousand years before the construction of the Tabernacle in Exodus. Thus, another assumption of the Documentary Hypothesis was exploded.

Wellhausen declared that the accounts of the patriarchs were written many hundreds of years later than is presented and that they reflected those later times. He stated the writers projected their creations back into antiquity.[88] Our knowledge of the history and cultures of the ancient Near East have also destroyed those assertions by Wellhausen. The patriarchal accounts accurately reflect the era which they claim to represent.[89] They do not reflect the later era from which Wellhausen and others claim them to have been written.

Other assumptions included that different diction, style and vocabulary indicate a different author; that too presumed accounts of the same event (such as the creation accounts in Genesis 1 and 2) are contradictory and from different authors; and that Israel's religion evolved from primitive animism through polytheism to eventual monotheism. The evidence undermines every one of Wellhausen's assumptions.

Wellhausen's division of the Pentateuch into four different authors designated these assumed authors by the letters J, E, D, & P. He added R for assumed editors or redactors who are alleged to have later put the separate writings together and added other details. He had to add a redactor in an effort to account for all the passages in the Pentateuch that contradict his theory despite his efforts to eliminate such evidence.

Distinguished Old Testament professor Walter Kaiser wrote that, *"No one has ever seen such J, E, D or P documents, or any allusion to them in any ancient literature ... Thus such hypothetical documents may be safely discounted in favor of real sources that are consistently referred to in the text, or are identified from epigraphic materials discovered in the ancient*

Near East."[90]

The Documentary Hypothesis was developed to provide an explanation of the Pentateuch that dismissed God as its source. It also sought to discredit Moses as its writer, reject its historicity, and destroy belief in its miracles. It was also intended to eliminate the witness to monotheism being the original religion of Israel. Wellhausen's speculations led to its intended conclusion among those indoctrinated in it over the past one hundred forty years.

The Documentary Hypothesis has convinced most theologians and mainline church pastors to assume that the Pentateuch is largely unreliable. Wellhausen declared, without any actual evidence, that parts of the Pentateuch were up to a thousand years after the events these writings deal with. This tactic successfully discredited the reliability of the text and of the events presented in the narratives. To repeat, this success is despite there not being a shred of manuscript or historical evidence in support of the theory.

If the Pentateuch had been actually written in the eighth century or later, as Wellhausen asserted, and not in its final form until the sixth century B.C. or later, we would expect the language to have reflected those later centuries. Since the primary language of the Near East including Israel was Aramaic from about the 10th through 6th centuries B.C., the Pentateuchal writings should reflect a heavy Aramaic influence if Wellhausen were correct.[91]

That is a reasonable expectation as the Biblical writings show considerable influence of the dominant surrounding nation's language and culture at the time the various documents were written. The Pentateuch shows the influence of early Babylonian and Egyptian language and culture – not Aramaic. The Pentateuch also fails to reflect the cultures of the Assyrian to Persian cultures that would be reflected in writings originating in the ninth to sixth centuries B.C.

The absence of these influences in the Pentateuch exposes the falsehood of this major assumption by Wellhausen. The Aramaic influence is mainly in writings during and after the Exile, such as in Daniel, Ezra, and Esther.

Those who follow Wellhausen claim the Old Testament including the Pentateuch was finally reaching the form familiar to us at the time Persia was the dominant cultural influence upon Judea. Yet, somehow, there is virtually no evidence of Persian influence on the Old Testament writings until during and after the exile.[92] This has to be an important conflict with the attempt to date the Pentateuch in this late period of history. To repeat, the Pentateuch does not show Persian influence in these writings.

In recent decades, English words have begun to appear more and more often within the vocabularies of other languages. This is because of the influence of the English-speaking nations in many fields such as international trade and finance. When I taught in China, one of my students stated that he had to learn English because all the textbooks in his field were written in English. These are examples of a dominant culture in an era influencing other languages.

As mentioned elsewhere, during Egypt's dominant influence on the Hebrews, we find numerous Egyptian words utilized in the Old Testament text. When the dominant influence changed to that of the Mesopotamian powers, Akkadian loanwords appear in the text of the Old Testament historical writings.[93]

During Judah's exile and restoration, we have the evidence of Persian loanwords in Biblical writings of that era, but not in the Pentateuch! So, if the Pentateuch was really written as late as Wellhausen asserted, why do they not reveal the similar use of Persian loanwords? They do not have Persian loanwords because the Pentateuch was written much earlier, during Babylonian and Egyptian dominance.

Bryant concludes, *"The Bible shows a small measure of linguistic influence from powerful foreign nations, so it is inexplicable that immersed as they were in Persian culture during the exile, the Jews would fail to reflect Persian loanwords in the Biblical text."* [94] The biblical writings made during the exile do reflect Persian influence as would be expected.

Wellhausen's reconstruction of the Old Testament and the history of Israel, involved a major rearrangement of the written documents and even larger misinterpretation or misrepresentation of the data. Like many liberals today, Wellhausen asserted what he wanted others to believe with scholarly explanations and detailed argument, but lacking any genuine objective evidence to support him.

If his theory were true, it would eliminate God as the source of the Pentateuch, and destroy belief in Moses as the human writer. Furthermore, the theory would discredit the entire Old Testament, destroy the credibility of Jesus, and eliminate the entire foundation for the Christian faith. [95]

Though false, the theory has done just that. This is an illegitimate undermining of the credibility of the foundational documents of the Old Testament. It has led to almost universal unbelief in the reliability of the Old Testament in the minds of those indoctrinated in it. This bogus portrayal of the Old Testament has been promoted as if true in Europe, Asia, and the U.S. by secular schools of religion and liberal Seminaries. The liberal mainstream churches and media promote the theory as well.

Challenges to Wellhausen's theory include that it violates the internal claims of the Pentateuch and eliminates the obvious unity of each of the five books. Also, the theory contradicts the obvious intention of the books to be taken as describing historical events. The evolutionary foundation for the Documentary Hypothesis is no longer credible and archaeology of the Near East completely discredits even the more recent variations of the theory.[96]

B.D. Eerdmans from the University of Leiden, *"asserted that it was impossible to use the divine names as evidence for separate documents."*[97] For one thing, there are often different names for God used in the same passage. In addition, archaeology has proven that in ancient times, gods and goddesses had multiple names or titles. The purpose of giving different names for God in varying situations was to indicate aspects of His nature and of His relating to humans in those differing circumstances.

Many sections of the Pentateuch are much too brief to establish different style and diction. Where such differences can be established, they are due to differing subject matter. The legal and ritual information in Leviticus would naturally differ in vocabulary and style from the narrative portions of Genesis as well as from the historical sections of Exodus.

Many ancient literary documents, whose unity of origin are beyond question, have major variations in style, vocabulary, and subject matter. If Wellhausen's ideas were applied to other literature it would quickly be seen how ridiculous the theory is. The value and credibility of any extensive literary writing would be destroyed by applying these methods to it.

G. Herbert Livingston makes this insightful statement

about Wellhausen's theory in <u>The Pentateuch In Its Cultural Environment</u>:

"Almost every book that promotes the theory has a listing of chapter and verses originally belonging to the independent documents. All isolated fragments that are left over are attributed, much too easily to redactors or compilers. It should be understood, however, that there are no literary references, no extant manuscripts of any kind, which mention the J, E, D, or P documents either singly or as a group. They have been created by separating them ... from the extant text of the Pentateuch."[98]

In other words, the Documentary Hypothesis though thoroughly accepted by most liberal Old Testament scholars, has absolutely no manuscript or historical evidence to support it; nothing! Wellhausen sliced the documents into segments according to his own subjective assumptions and then asserted the results he himself has created are evidence supporting his theory. Such treatment of documents would be rejected as ludicrous if it were not the basis for rejecting the reliability of the Old Testament.

Reality contrasts sharply with the fiction promoted by the Documentary Hypothesis. Archaeologist W.F. Albright wrote regarding the Pentateuch that *"New discoveries continue to confirm the historical accuracy or the literary antiquity of detail after detail in it."*[99]

An argument used in support of the Documentary Hypothesis is that it accounts for alleged contradictions and variations in parallel accounts in the Pentateuch. However, when you read the narratives as actually written, it is obvious that most of the assumed parallel accounts are actually records of separate events that occurred at different times.

A primary example of this is the two cases of Abraham

54

and one of Isaac, attempting to pass off their wives as their sisters. They did this out of fear for their own safety. (Genesis 12;11-18; 20:2-13 26:6-11). Abraham's faith failed twice in regard to concern for his own safety and his son later followed the example of his father.

In addition, ancient scribes often retold events from different perspectives. For example, the charge that the Creation in Genesis 2 contradicts that of chapter 1 is instead an example of normal ancient practice. Chapter 1 presents the cosmic or global overall perspective, while chapter 2 focuses in on a more limited and anthropocentric perspective.[100]

W.F. Albright wrote in his <u>Archaeology Confronts Biblical Criticism</u> that Wellhausen's *"standpoint is antiquated and its picture of the early evolution of Israel is sadly distorted."* [101] However, the Documentary Hypothesis lives on because it gives the appearance of justifying the evolution of Israel's religion and seems to validate rejection of the reliability of the Old Testament.

Jewish author Herman Wouk analyzes Wellhausen's tomb in some detail in his notes at the end of his excellent book <u>This Is My God</u>. An excerpt from his perceptive remarks on Wellhausen's methodology follows:

"His method is simple, but the working out in detail is grandiose. Whatever passages of scripture support his thesis, or at least do not oppose it, are authentic. Wherever the text contradicts him, the verses are spurious. His attack on each verse that does not support him is violent. He shows bad grammar, or internal inconsistency, or corrupt vocabulary, or jerkiness of continuity, every time. There is no passage he cannot explain away or annihilate. If he has to change the plain meaning of Hebrew words, he

does that too. He calls this 'conjectural emendation.'"
102

Wouk's remarks indicate the extreme bias with which Wellhausen approached the Biblical scriptures. Wellhausen was willing to do and claim anything necessary to justify his destructive critical perspective, including altering the obvious meaning of the Hebrew words. That is not legitimate scholarship, but perversely twisting the tools of scholarship to justify his preconceived purpose.

Wouk adds that if one wants to read Wellhausen's Prolegomena, *"It should be read Bible in hand so that one can watch the professor at work making his crazy-quilt scriptures. Without knowing Hebrew, one cannot see the liberties he takes with the ancient tongue, but the chopping and changing are plain enough for the most part in English."*[103]

Many scholars have presented evidence and reasoning that thoroughly demolishes any basis for Wellhausen's theory. This was accomplished soon after the theory was published as well as continuing today. Even when comparing the actual texts, as spliced up segments, one can often see the questionable validity of Wellhausen's fabrications. The flow of the context often contradicts the theory. Not only that, but, the arbitrary and artificial efforts to create separate documents, is frequently apparent to one not blinded by the theory.

Reading the scholars' reasons for rejecting his theories, we can see very quickly that when liberals or other skeptics are speaking or writing about the Bible, facts are often surrendered to theories and imagination. It becomes obvious that when reality contradicts their views, they often reject reality. This is the opposite of genuine scholarship, as Kenneth Kitchen stated, *"Priority must always be given to tangible, objective data, and to external evidence over subjective theory or speculative opinions. Facts must control theory, not vice versa."* [104]

Wellhausen revealed both his extreme subjectivity and biases when he wrote that *"I learned through Ritschl that Karl Heinrich Graf placed the Law later than the prophets, and, almost without knowing his reasons for the hypothesis, I was prepared to accept it; I readily acknowledged to myself the possibility of understanding Hebrew antiquity without the book of the Torah."* [105]

It is difficult to imagine a serious scholar stating that the Torah (the Pentateuch) was not essential to understanding Hebrew history and culture! The Torah provides the foundation for the history and culture of Judaism, as well as for the remainder of the Old Testament itself. It is also quite telling that Wellhausen was willing to accept Graf's theories without knowing any of the reasoning behind it!

Like so much modern theology and religion, Wellhausen's hypothesis is purely the creation of men's imaginings, preferences, and assertions. In this case, the critics reject the Biblical narratives as unreliable even though there is extensive evidence verifying it. Yet, they accept the documentary hypothesis without any evidence to support the confirmation of it and though it has been thoroughly disproven and discredited.

In fact, despite its complete lack of credibility, there are recent attempts, to exhume and more widely promote the theory. Scholars who want the theory to be true revise and revise. Their revisions are quite superficial and do not resolve the contradictions in the theory with our knowledge of the cultural and historical realities. A parallel case would be to continually tear down and rebuild structures on an unstable and seriously insecure foundation. It is the foundation itself that needs to be replaced and then rebuild. The anti-supernatural and anti-biblical assumptions are the flawed foundation. for the theory.

"Who Wrote the Bible?" by Richard Elliot Friedman is an example of these attempts to make the theory seem plausible. For instance, Friedman makes the incredible statement, *"Thus the Wellhausen model began to answer the question of why different sources existed."*[106]

As mentioned, in reality, there are no actual sources, but these are assumed because they are needed. The so called 'different sources' are created by slicing up the actual documents that we possess into segments according to the theory. There has never been any evidence of source documents for the Documentary Hypothesis. Whatever is needed to substantiate the theory is merely assumed, created by its proponents, and asserted to be evidence as Friedman himself does.

More recently Friedman has written and stated, that, *"The Documentary Hypothesis is still the most common view in scholarship, and no other model has a comparable consensus, but in the end the question is not a matter of consensus anyway. It is a matter of evidence. And the evidence for the hypothesis is, in my judgement, now substantial and stronger than ever."* [107]

It is true that the hypothesis is the most common view, but that is because most current scholars have been indoctrinated in it. It also has the consensus of scholars because it justifies their preferences. Friedman's claim that the evidence supports the theory is scholarly devised fiction.

Friedman briefly states six arguments justifying the Documentary process of dividing up the text of the Pentateuch according to the assumptions of the

58

theory. Then he concludes that, *"The most compelling argument for the hypothesis is that this hypothesis best accounts for the fact that all this evidence of so many kinds [mentioned above] comes together so consistently."* [108]

The arguments Friedman refers to are 'Linguistic,' 'Consistency of Content,' 'Continuity of Text,' 'Connections With Other Parts of the Bible' and 'Relationships Among the Sources.'[109] Most of those arguments could be used more appropriately to justify the integrity of each of the books of the Pentateuch as completed by one author. Read each of the books of the Pentateuch through, as written. That will demonstrate that there is no need or justification to divide up the content of any of the books as if written by multiple authors.

The theory is assumed and asserted to be true and the evidence is then created from applying the theory to the documents to justify it. The documents are divided up to agree with the theory and therefore have a superficial semblance of justifying it. Each argument is dependent upon first accepting the theory to be true and then creating the evidence to make it appear to be true. This is the ultimate example of reasoning in a circle.[110]

But since history, archaeology and anthropology have disproven the theory, the literary arguments have no merit or significance regardless of how valid they may seem. It is like assuming the ridiculous idea or theory that a circle is actually a triangle. The theory would have to be true for any argument in support of it to be valid no matter how well thought out and detailed the presentation might be.

Friedman has not presented any actual evidence that could refute the historical and other evidence that the theory is false, so he is playing with words. Friedman has, as do all documentarians, created the only apparent evidence for the theory from the extant text. He divides the text consistently, according to the theoretical assumptions, and then declares how amazing it is that the evidence is consistent.

Friedman admits that some contend the theory was disproven long ago, which it was. He continues that now, *"The most common challenges have come from a number of European scholars, but as of this time, they have not responded to the central evidence. Specifically: they have not come to terms with the linguistic evidence, the continuity of the sources (especially J and E) with history or the convergence of the lines of evidence."*

As mentioned previously, there is no genuine 'continuity with history' in the hypothesis. One must first accept the theory and the late dates required by the theory as well as ignoring the contrary evidence for both. Perhaps those European scholars have discovered it is futile to present evidence to documentarians like Friedman who are so enamored with what they have created. Friedman attempts to write convincingly yet still without any evidence other than the biased suppositions and conjectures of scholars unwilling to face the authenticity and credibility of the Old Testament scriptures.

Arnold and Beyer state for instance that, *"studies suggest that ancient Near Eastern literary traditions were often recorded in writing soon after the events they describe, not centuries later."* [111] This would contradict claims of skeptics and documentarians that the records were written at least hundreds of years after the events. The critics need to create the illusion of a great time lapse in order to justify their other attacks on the Bible's credibility.

Even the comparison of other ancient Near Eastern

literature reveals the questionable validity of Wellhausen's assumptions. There are obvious examples of one author using a variety of styles within the same document. The Egyptians often used different names for people groups and different names for the same city and objects. Speaking of Egyptian practice, Historian Edwin Yamauchi explains that these word variations do not indicate differing sources or authors. *"Not only were various synonyms used but various styles were employed in a single document."*[112]

There are several other methods of Biblical criticism applied to the study of the Old Testament in additional to the Documentary Hypothesis. These various methods can occasionally provide insight, but must be compared and evaluated in light of control data, such as ancient Near Eastern historical data and other ancient Near Eastern literature.[113] Literary analysis without control data can often degenerate into the promotion of subjective conjecture and personal preferences rather than valid insights.

"Cyrus Gordon points out that the principles of the theory would lead to palpable absurdities if exercised in the study of Ugaritic, Egyptian or Akkadian literatures."[114]

If one were to apply the various assumptions of the Documentary Hypothesis to Friedman's own writings that would likely prove he was not the author of much of his own material. Differences in subject matter, vocabulary and diction would show perhaps as many as three or four other actual writers. The theory is absurd.

Internal Evidence of Moses' Authorship

Historian Edwin Yamauchi has written, *"It is an indication of the authentic character of Genesis that whereas 1-36 betray their Mesopotamian background, Genesis 37-50, the story of Joseph, reveals an intimate knowledge of Egypt.*"[115]

To recount briefly, earlier it was mentioned that significant evidence of the historicity of the Pentateuch is the obvious Egyptian background of these writings. The earliest chapters of Genesis reflect the early Babylonian influence. The remainder of the Pentateuch reveals a strong Egyptian impact. That Egyptian influence would not exist were someone writing these accounts hundreds of years later as critics maintain.

That the geography of Egypt and Sinai is well known by the author, has been confirmed by archaeology. Egyptian words are much more common than in other portions of the Old Testament and Egyptian names are frequent. [116] Canaan is compared to Egypt and references are worded as if the author and people have not yet been there.

For example, mentioning Shalem, *"a city of Shechem, which is in the land of Canaan"* is not the way a writer would refer to a land the people had been dwelling in for hundreds of years. All of this is as would be expected if authored by one raised in the Egyptian court as was Moses who never was in Canaan.[117]

There are also cultural references and specific words in Genesis that verify its accuracy and age because they became obsolete and unknown hundreds of years later.[118] The skeptics are proven wrong through literary analysis of the vocabulary of the Pentateuch, if one ignores the critic's prior assumptions and assertions.

It is obvious that most of Exodus as well as Leviticus and Numbers are directed to a people involved in wilderness wanderings, *"not a nation of farmers settled for centuries in their promised land."* [119]

Detailed instructions for marching and encampment and other details show they are in the desert and frequently on the move.[120]

When it is asserted that Moses is the author or writer of the Pentateuch, it is not intended to mean that he wrote every word of those documents. For one thing, he is likely to have been making use of some earlier writings. Abraham was from a highly civilized city in early Babylon where writing had been practiced for hundreds of years. As a wealthy merchant, he undoubtedly wrote and kept records. He very well may have passed down some written records of earlier history and culture as well as that of his own time.[121]

There are also some cases where later writers or editors added comments to the Mosaic writings. Moses' obituary at the end of Deuteronomy would be a major example of a later addition. So would the comment about Moses' humility and later updating of place names for recognition.

What evidence exists that would indicate Moses was actually the author of the Pentateuch? There are clear statements of Moses authorship within the writings. See Exodus 17:14; 24:4, 7; 34:27; Numbers 33:2; Deuteronomy 31:9, 19, 22, 24. Also, *"speeches of God are frequently introduced with such phrases as 'The Lord spoke to Moses saying.'"* [122] (Exodus 25:1; Leviticus 4:1).

As Arnold and Beyer mention it is also significant that *"in fact most of the material from Exodus through Deuteronomy relates to the life and ministry of Moses in one form or another. Moses was the central historical figure during the period that Exodus – Deuteronomy describes. This fact, in conjunction with all the internal evidence, led to nearly uncontested tradition of mosaic authorship of the Pentateuch."*[123] That was true until the modern era when some skeptical writers began to attempt to undermine the authority of scripture.

There are also frequent statements throughout the Old Testament of Moses authorship. Examples include: Joshua 8:31-32; 1 Kings 2:3; 2 Kings 14:6; 21:8; 2 Chronicles 35:6; Ezra 6:18; Nehemiah 8:1; 9:14; 10:29; 13:1; Daniel 9:11-13; Malachi 4:4.

Consistent Jewish written tradition links Moses to these documents. The Talmud calls them *"the books of Moses."*[124] The Mishna and first century Jewish historian, Josephus presents Moses as the author as well.[125] Skeptics ignore or discount such evidence.

There are several statements of Jesus indicating that Moses was the author. *"All things which are written of me in the Law of Moses, and the prophets and the Psalms must be fulfilled."* (Luke 24:44) *"For if you believed Moses, you would believe me; for he wrote of me. But if you will not believe his writings, how will you believe my words?"* (John 5:46-47). *"Did not Moses give you the law, and yet none of you carries out the Law?"* (John 7:19, 22). The historical evidence supports Moses as the writer of the Pentateuch.

When the biblical Scriptures are rejected as the revelation of God; theories, conjectures, contradictions, and unfounded assumptions and opinions multiply. There is absolutely no basis for any of the speculations of the Documentary Hypothesis. Only a determined anti-supernatural bias can account for such credulity and imagination the proponents of the theory are willing to promote.

Refutation Of Specific Old Testament Criticisms

Genesis chapters 1 and 2 are declared by critics to be two different and contradictory creation accounts. One criticism is that chapter 1 has plants and birds created prior to humans, whereas chapter 2 reverses the order. Chapter 1 actually lists the sequence of creation. Chapter 2 does not present an ordered sequence of creative events as chapter 1 does. Chapter 2 relates other living things to the centrality of the creation of man.

Chapter 2 merely mentions the plants after mentioning the creation of man. There is no necessity of seeing chapter 2 as presenting a sequence of events. Also, the Hebrew verb in chapter 2:19 is not a present tense like in English. It refers to completed action and can be translated, *"had formed"*[126] which would refer to a prior event. [127] The plant life and animals were created previously. Then after creating man, God brings the animals to see what the man would call them.

Another criticism is that 1:27 has Adam and Eve being created at the same time while chapter 2 has Eve created later. Chapter 1 does not give a specific timing merely specifying that both were created by God on the same day.

Actually, chapter 2 is presenting a more detailed portrayal of one aspect of the overall creation account of chapter 1. *"The creation of humanity is the climax of chapter 1 but the centerpiece of chapter 2."*[128] There is no contradiction, but a contrast in purpose between the two passages. They are not separate accounts.

One skeptic wrote that following eating the forbidden fruit in Genesis 3, *"Instead of invoking the death sentence promised earlier, God curses the man to a life of hard work."* [129] The critic does not seem to recognize that God is not talking primarily about physical death, although that also resulted later from the disobedience. God was speaking of spiritual death. Jesus told Nicodemus that he must be born again, or born, from above. That means that some essential aspect or part of Nicodemus was not alive. Ephesians

2:1-5 mentions that believers were dead in our sins and trespasses prior to coming to Christ, and that we have been made alive in Christ.

Genesis 4:21-22 are claimed by skeptics to be errors because they say humans were not advanced enough that early in history to create musical instruments and forge iron and bronze. How would the skeptics know that?

These are unprovable assumptions based upon the belief that early humans were primitive, lacking the knowledge and skills necessary for such creativity. However, even the first humans revealed high intelligence in naming all the animals, their ability to express themselves and their self-awareness (Gen. 2:18-25; 3:1-13; 4:1).

Genesis 5:1 and 6:9 are cited as proof Moses didn't write Genesis. Now that we know writing existed long before Moses, there is no reason to think that he could not be referencing earlier written documents in these and other places. That does not refute that he is the author of Genesis. I cite many other writers in my books, but I am the author of those books.

Genesis 12:6 is assumed by a critic to indicate that the Canaanites have been removed from the land, which did not occur until over four hundred years later. However, the statement reads *"Now the Canaanite was then in the land."* This is merely an acknowledgement of one group that was living in the land at that time. Those words do not suggest that they have been removed.

Gen. 14:14 is said to be a mistake because there was no such person as Dan the son of Jacob until hundreds of years later and therefore there would be no city of Dan named for him. Dan is from a common Hebrew root meaning to judge or rule. Though a city named Dan may have existed in Abraham's time, long before the later invasion of Canaan by the tribes of Israel; this is likely to be a later updating of place names for convenience and understanding.

Another alleged contradiction is in regard to the wives of Esau. The skeptics declare the lists conflict. Gen. 26:34 and 28:9 list his known wives as Hittites, Judith, the daughter of Beeri, and Basemath, the daughter of Elon, and then Mahalath, the daughter of Ishmael. Gen. 36:2-3 however, lists Esau's wives as Adah, daughter of Elon, Oholibamah, daughter of Anah, and Basemath, Ismael's daughter.

The second list is recounting Esau's generations, so Judith is not mentioned because she apparently bore no children. In addition, people were often known by more than one name.[130] Basemath, daughter of Elon, was apparently also known as Adah and was so listed to distinguish her from Basemath, daughter of Ishmael. [131] Oholibamah was an additional wife married later perhaps because Judith was barren. There is no actual problem.

Genesis 36:31 states *"Now these are the kings who reigned in the land of Edom before any king reigned over the sons of Israel."* This is claimed to prove someone much later than Moses wrote because it refers to kings ruling Israel nearly seven hundred years before they had a king. Actually, God had told Abraham and Sarah long before Moses time that they would have descendants who would be kings (Genesis 17:6, 15-19). There is no discrepancy because Moses knew of that earlier prediction though the fulfillment was still in the future.

It is claimed to be an error that Joseph is written to have stated, *"I was kidnapped from the land of the Hebrews"* (Gen. 40:15). Much earlier Abram is called a Hebrew (Gen. 14:13) and that he was considered a mighty prince in the land (Gen. 23:6). God had promised this land to him and his descendants (Gen. 13:14-15). For two more full generations Abraham's descendants lived in the land. Potiphar's wife also called Joseph a Hebrew (Gen. 39:14, 17). For each of these reasons it is not unreasonable for Joseph to have considered his homeland to be the land of the Hebrews.

Another example of the careless statements of many critics is this statement of John Barton in the Anchor Bible Commentary: *"Numbers 25 describes the rebellion at Peor and refers to the Moabite women, the next sentence says the women were Midianites."*[132]

Actually, the reference to the Midianite women occurs five verses later (Num. 25:6). While the people are grieving the sin and judgement from the prior involvement with Moabite women, one Israelite brings into their camp a Midianite woman. These are different women and different events. This is clearly a separate situation that occurred near the previous one. There is no connection between the women and no contradiction.

Criticism has been made that in Deut. 3:14 the Trans-Jordon region is said to be called Havoth-Jair after Jair, the son of Manasseh, though the area was not named this until later. Havoth-Jair means 'villages of Jair.' Actually, it was so named by Jair. The fact that it refers to the prior name of the area is no argument against it being known as designated in Deut. 3:14 following Jair's conquest. Jair ruled Israel during the time of the Judges (Judges 10:3-5).

Another frequent practice of skeptics is to lift a verse or passage out of its literary context, thus distorting the information and then claiming it to be false and proof the Bible is unreliable. Context means the other surrounding information that indicates how the specific words are being used. The context determines the actual meaning of the passage. Another use of phrases or verses out of context is to compare one passage to other information that it appears to contradict.

The apparent contradiction is created by the skeptic because of ignoring the intent of the larger passage. Sometimes both references being used to create the appearance of a contradiction or discrepancy are being used contrary to their actual meaning.

Another example of this tactic is to contrast information from different historical or cultural situations as if the two situations are the same and should exactly agree. The critic then pretends this is a discrepancy in the Bible.

Instead of a problem in the Bible, this practice is a discrepancy in scholarly methodology which if used in regard to other literature, would make the other writings self-contradictory and unintelligible. It is not used in regard to other literature, however, because the purpose of the tactic is not to discover truth, but to dissuade people from believing the Biblical scriptures.

Another tactic of skeptics which I have referred to in other writings, is to use sarcastic humor as a substitute for logic or evidence. Bertrand Russel was skilled at this subterfuge. For example, in 2 Samuel 24, David has a census taken particularly to know the complete size of his available army. God brings a plague in judgement for this intent to rely upon the size of his army instead of relying upon God. Russel states that the Lord, who hated statistics, brought a plague upon Israel. Russel's intent is to make God seem ridiculous.

The actual issue here is an apparent contradiction between the numbers of troops in the parallel account in 1 Chronicles 21:5-6. The Samuel account lists the army as 800,000 for Israel and 500,000 for Judah. The numbers in Chronicles gives 1,100,000 for Israel and 470,000 for Judah. The resolution is that Samuel did not include the regular standing army of 288,000 for Israel, mentioned in 1 Chron. 27:1-15 nor the 12,000 assigned to Jerusalem in the same way, 2 Chronicles 14. The 470,000 in 1 Chron. 21 did not include the 30,000 in the regular army of Judah mentioned in 2 Samuel 6:1. So each record is correct depending upon the groups included or excluded. Also, the 1 Chron. 21 account mentions Joab didn't complete the totals for Judah.[133].

External Confirmation

The first two criteria for evaluating ancient documents, the Bibliographic and Internal Evidence, establish that we have an authentic and reliable text of the Old Testament. This moves us to the second vital question to be answered. Knowing the document's text is authentic and genuine does not prove that the information is true. The question that external evidence attempts to answer is whether there is sufficient reliable evidence outside the Bible itself to verify that the information which has been accurately transmitted to us in the Old Testament is also actually true.

Though the text is authentic and reliable, with supposed peoples and events of such a long time ago, how can we know whether these things really happened? It also needs to be reemphasized that the historical reliability or factuality of the information presented is considered vital.

This is an important question to be resolved with evidence and logic. Many merely dismiss the Bible as the same as other non-historical writings without any consideration of the evidence that would disprove such assumptions. The non-believing scholars and

70

other critics generally assume the Old Testament is filled with myth and legend. Fortunately, there is significant information that indicates the Bible is far beyond any of those other writings in authenticity and reliability.

C.S. Lewis was earlier quoted as saying he would like to know how many fables and myths these critics have really studied, not how much time they have spent studying the Biblical text. He spent his entire career reading and teaching myths and fables and said the Bible is not at all like those types of writings.

It might also be asked, as some do, what difference it makes whether or not the Old Testament is historically true or not. Such scholars tell us that what is important is the moral or spiritual lessons we can draw from these stories, rather than their being actual accounts of real events. Does it really matter whether the events recorded are genuine historical records?

Yes, as a matter of fact it matters very much. Jesus referred to Moses, David, Jonah, and their writings as factual. He referred to events in the Old Testament as if they actually happened. If He were mistaken then we have nothing reliable upon which to base the Christian Faith, and no reason to trust in what else He taught.

Steven Masood stated in The Bible and the Qu'ran: A Question of Integrity, that, *"Jesus accepted the integrity of the Old Testament books. In his teaching and preaching he referred to them as scripture (John 5:39; Matthew 21:42; 22:29; 26:54; Luke 4:21; 24:27; Mark 12:10). It is on his authority that Christians accept the validity of the Old Testament."* [134]

Jesus' authority and accuracy is of vital significance. Whether or not the historicity or historical reliability of these documents can be verified is very important because the Christian Faith is based upon the actuality of specific historical events. It is a uniquely historical faith. If these events did not occur than the Christian Faith is untrue and a fraud. If they are true then the Christian Faith is the unique truth about God and his relating to humanity.

However, vast numbers of the events recorded in the scriptures can be shown to be historically true. That makes this collection of writings something to be taken very seriously indeed. It is of great significance because the book claims to be a record of God's dealing with people throughout history; as preparation for His work to redeem fallen humanity.

These Biblical writings also purport to inform us of our meaning, significance, and purpose for existing and our destiny. And if Biblical writings are true, then according to the law of non-contradiction, all religious scriptures and other writings that fail to agree with the Bible are necessarily false.

There are other reasons to be concerned with the information in the Old Testament as well. Without the Old Testament we would be missing at least two-thirds of the story of God's dealing with humanity and the background for understanding most of the New Testament. This includes answers to fundamental questions as to the origin of the universe and humanity, the purpose and meaning of existence, the origin of evil and its solution, etc.

We would know nothing about the fulfillment of Old Testament prophecy including the predictions of the coming of the Messiah and His purposes. In addition, the Bible has answers to the fundamental questions that people have wrestled with for millennia.

Another evidence of the Old Testament's reliability and trustworthiness is the Bible's avoidance of the mythologies and misperceptions prevalent in the cultures at the times the various books were written.

The Babylonian and Sumerian creation accounts closely parallel much of the Genesis account except that they add the mythical elements of many gods arguing and fighting over decisions and their gross immorality, etc. Critics ignore these significant differences and try to use these other creation accounts to discredit the Biblical record.

Though the Old Testament writers are aware of the mythologies of their neighbors and mention it, they never believe it and never advocate nor encourage it. Also, in regard to mythology, the Jews knew their God was active in their history and lives. Contrary to pagan religion, the Jews knew God could not be manipulated into doing something just because of the performance of some ritual or liturgy.

Mythology was completely foreign to the Hebrew mind. Faith was in a personal God who had already acted in history on their behalf and would again do so according to His divine purposes, not as a result of being coerced by some magical formula as the pagans believed.

The account of Noah and the flood are in Genesis chapters 6-8. Some critics divide the narrative into two separate accounts so as to give the illusion there are contradictions in the narrative. One critic remarks that, *"it is significant that it is possible to separate the text into two continuous stories like this."* [135] He then states that even more significant is that this can be done throughout the Pentateuch. Scholarly skeptics often go to great lengths to create fabricated evidence that appears to support their unbelief.

The alleged significance, however, is created by that author. You can divide the narrative into two separate accounts if you want to and if you intend to create an illusion that there were originally two accounts that contradict each other. Establishing your methods on how to divide the original narrative will determine how many contradictions you can create out of your fiction.

The reality is that there have never been any documents or other evidence that there were originally two accounts of the flood. The supposed evidence is all fabricated in the skeptics' mind and worked out in detail to give the illusion that it is reliable.

After dividing the accounts, they present their arguments for the division which are all based upon their previous assumptions. They pretend that their arguments to justify the division is evidence in support of their assumptions.

We could use the same procedure of selective division and editing on their own writings to prove that they seriously contradict themselves and that many of their writings were actually authored by others.

Despite the voluminous writings explaining, detailing, and justifying such distortions of the text, the argument has no validity. The eagerness of the skeptic to accept such nonsense shows how their presuppositions make them susceptible to embrace almost any argument that superficially seems to validate those preferences. It is all very subjective.

Another argument of critics has been that the absence of references to the Levitical (ceremonial) law *"from Joshua to the exile"* proves it did not exist until after the exile. [136] They refer especially to the following references as evidence in this regard: Isa. 1:11-15; Jer. 7:21-23; Amos 5:21-25; Micah 6:6-8. These very references each refer to the ceremonial practices and that God rejects the performance of these rituals because they are meaningless due to Israel's idolatry and ignoring of the more important moral law.

It is evident that the references also show that the moral law was given prior to the ceremonial law indicating its priority. In addition, the creation of the Tabernacle in Moses time and the Temple built by Solomon much later are based upon the reality of the Levitical practices. [137] Notice that none of the references used by the critics deny the existence of the ceremonial law. Those very references used by the critics destroy their argument.

Gleason Archer one of the greatest of recent Old Testament scholars wrote: *"Judging therefore by the internal evidences of the Pentateuchal text, we are driven to the conclusion that the author must have been originally a resident of Egypt (not of Palestine), a contemporary eyewitness of the Exodus and wilderness wandering, and possessing of a very high degree of education, learning and literary skill."* [138]

A master of 45 languages, including all those related to the Old Testament eras, Robert Dick Wilson wrote, *"I may add that the result of my forty five years of study of the Bible has led me all the time to a firmer faith that in the Old Testament we have a true historical account of the history of the Israelite people."*[139]

External Confirmation From Archaeology

Next we are to consider in much more detail, the third criteria for evaluating ancient documents, that of external confirmation. So, is there any external evidence substantial enough to demonstrate that the Biblical scriptures are historically accurate? As a matter of fact, there is. There is so much evidence. So much archaeological and historical data, we could easily write multiple books just presenting the evidence for the historical accuracy of the New Testament.

And contrary to some very outspoken religion scholars, the mainstream media, and popular misunderstanding, there is also a wealth of information documenting the historical reliability of the Old Testament as well. This is despite its different books having been written from 400 to 1900 years earlier than the New Testament.

There are two types of confirmation of the Bible through archaeology. There is the obvious case, where some discovery verifies a specific person, event, or other detail of Scripture. The second type is where there is no specific allusion, but the presentation in the Scriptures is consistent with the culture and characteristics of a particular time and place.

Skeptics repudiate and scoff at the opening chapters of Genesis as merely another version of ancient mythology. They ignore the obvious differences in the Biblical accounts from the mythological versions declaring that there is no basis in fact.

However, some scholars studying the most ancient Chinese pictographs known, have come to different conclusions. Their research has shown that these Chinese records from antiquity agree in an amazing degree with the first chapters of Genesis regarding origins. [140] Through their detailed analysis, we now have outside corroboration of the Genesis creation accounts that lack the mythology, polytheism, and additional distortions of other non-Biblical accounts!

Archaeological discoveries have shown that the stories of the Patriarchs in Genesis accurately reflect the culture of those times. These cultural practices would not have been known to authors writing many hundreds of years later as critics assert. The accuracy of minor cultural details reveals the Pentateuch is not the garbled paste job Wellhausen and others have made it out to be.

In addition, the famous W.F. Albright and others have shown that so called advanced ideas of one universal God was prevalent throughout the ancient Near East prior to two thousand B.C.[141] This eliminates support for contentions that Israel's monotheism evolved into existence in 700 B.C. or later. The Pentateuch was written, about 1450 B.C. and clearly teaches monotheism; that there is only one true God.

Albright also wrote that on the basis of archaeology, including his own discoveries, that, *"as a whole the picture in Genesis is historical, and there is no reason to doubt the general accuracy of the biographical details and the sketches of personality which make the Patriarchs come alive with a vividness unknown to a single extra-Biblical character in the whole vast literature of the ancient Near East."* [142] These archaeological discoveries completely reversed Albright's prior rejection of the historical reliability of Genesis and the rest of the Old Testament.

A recent article by Professor Nahum Sarna points out that the antiquity and authenticity of the Patriarchal narratives are confirmed at many points by other Near Eastern documents of that era. Not only that, but as he informs us, these cultural phenomena contradict those of later times. [143] Thus, the evidence in the narratives themselves refute the claims of critics, that these writings were much later inventions, projected back into earlier times.

Ancient Near Eastern contracts have been discovered that reveal the accuracy of legal and social backgrounds that are portrayed at the time of the Patriarchs.[144] J.A. Thompson explains that, *"in many of the passages in the Old Testament which describe the establishment or the renewal of the covenant between Yahweh and Israel, there is a literary pattern which closely follows that found in the treaties of the ancient Near East.*"[145] For example, see Exodus 20:1-17 a Biblical narrative which follows the ancient pattern.

The treaty agreements between Abraham and Abimelech (Gen. 21:22ff); Abraham and the Hittites (Gen. 23) show the cultural appropriateness of the Biblical records in this regard.

Rights of inheritance are an example of Moses accurately presenting legal practices. It was stipulated in the Law of Moses that a double inheritance was to be given to the firstborn son (Duet. 21:15-17). Critics have pointed out that Near East texts of 2000 B.C. stipulate an equal share for each heir. However, the eighteen-fifteenth century texts from Mari and Nuzi indicate a double share be given a natural firstborn son. So, Moses' stipulation was consistent with the cultural changes of the time that he was writing.[146]

Critics have attempted to devalue the Pentateuch by emphasizing the similarities between it and the code of Hammurabi. However, as Donald Demaray points out, *"The similarities between the Mosaic and the Hammurabi codes is explained by the universal similarity of crimes, but the whole atmosphere of the Hebrew Law is more humane than that of the Babylonian."* [147] Examples are that Hammarabi prescribes various forms of bodily mutilation for some crimes as well as unlimited floggings. Mutilation is absent from the Mosaic Law and flogging is limited.[148]

Perhaps you have wondered or been asked to explain why most historians and many religion professors ignore or deny the historical validity of the Old Testament scriptures if the evidence is so supportive. The following extensive quote from Richard Purtill's textbook, *Thinking About Religion*, summarizes the type and quality of information and then explains why this is so frequently ignored by scholars:

"It is sometimes claimed that historians simply as historians regard the Old and New Testament history as unreliable on some independent historical grounds. But actually ... Many events which are regarded as firmly established historically have far less documentary evidence than many Biblical events, and the documents on which historians rely for much secular history are written much longer after the events than many records of Biblical events.

"Furthermore we have many more copies of Biblical narratives than of secular histories, and the surviving copies are much earlier than those on which our evidence for secular history is based. If the Biblical narratives did not contain accounts of miraculous events or have reference to God ... Biblical history would probably be regarded as much more firmly established than most of the history of say, Classical Greece and Rome." [149]

Purtill continues:

"But because the Biblical accounts do mention miracles and do involve reference to God ... considerations other than purely historical come into the picture. Some historians are convinced as part of their general worldview that miracles don't happen and that there is no spiritual world." [150]

It is very important to note what he has written. In other words, it is not the unreliability of the Biblical records or contradictory manuscripts that accounts for the refusal to consider the historicity of the Biblical documents. It is the refusal to even consider the evidence, because it conflicts with their anti-supernatural bias and presuppositions.

Most critics never bother to consult the evidence though it is extensive because it conflicts with their worldview. Their anti-supernatural bias causes them to assume God does not exist, miracles cannot happen and that is the end of the issue for them.

A different issue is that some of the professing experts on the Bible who deny its reliability make statements they know are untrue. They apparently assume most people will not know the difference between merely asserting that something is true and genuine evidence that it is true.

Remember that critics declared there were no such people as the Hittites until archaeology uncovered that civilization along with a huge library of Hittite writings in Turkey.[151] Most skeptics are interested in appearing to seek truth but truth is usually very secondary to them. They are primarily concerned with developing and maintaining their reputation and income as intellectually skeptical scholars at universities and liberal religious institutions.

Let's examine in detail a special example of the historical evidence for the Old Testament from Genesis, one of the oldest Old Testament books. Genesis 14 is one of the most controversial and criticized chapters in the Old Testament because of all its historical references. The date for Abraham's migration to Canaan from Ur varies from about 2000 to 1800 B.C. I assume it was about 1900 B.C. or earlier. I'll summarize the information in Chapter 14. Read it carefully yourself.

In 14:1-7 we are told that a confederation of four kings from Elam and other nearby city states take a specific route down into Palestine conquering and re-conquering cities as they travel down. These kings were reinvading because these cities and the kings in Palestine had apparently rebelled against one of the

Northern kings.

In 14:8-12 a confederation of five kings in Southern Palestine gather their troops to fight the Northern kings but the Southern Alliance loses the battle. Many people, livestock and goods are captured, by the Northern Alliance, including the people's food supply and Abraham's nephew, Lot. Then the triumphant Northern kings begin their trek back to their homeland.

In 14:13-16, 24 Abraham is alerted to what has happened, and goes in pursuit of the Northern kings with his own 317 hired servants and three allies. They defeat the Northern kings and return with the former captives and all the goods. A great story, but did it really happen? Is this a genuinely historical event? Is there any way to prove this really happened?

William Foxwell Albright was considered the greatest American Archaeologist of the past generation and it has been written concerning him that *"Albright made Palestinian Archaeology into a science."* This is no mere novice. Initially, he and other critics gave five reasons why the chapter was obviously unhistorical and merely legendary:

1. He declared that the kings listed in the chapter were not historical persons.

2. He stated that military Confederations did not exist that early in history.

3. He said there was no evidence travel was that extensive until much later.

4. He said that the cities cited in the chapter were unhistorical and that there was no travel route in the area mentioned in Genesis. These two were *"the best proof of the essentially legendary character of the narrative."*[152]

5. He stated that it was impossible for Abraham and a few servants to defeat an army that had supposedly

defeated a military alliance of five kings.

Albright declared that this was proof that the Old Testament was not a reliable book historically. Critics of the Bible were undoubtedly elated. It looked very bad for the Bible's reputation and reliability for a while. But notice that each of the five objections to the reliability of the Bible account is based upon the absence of information, not from an evaluation of available data.

Up to that time, there was no information available outside of the Genesis account of any of these locations or persons. Such criticisms and rejection of the Biblical record by opponents of the Christian Faith are very common. The criticisms are based upon assumptions that the Bible could not be reliable since there is no outside confirmation. The arguments were not based upon any actual evidence.

This is a typical method of Bible critics. When there is no information outside the Bible about a person, place, or event, it is assumed and declared that the Bible is wrong, that the passages are merely mythical or legendary. When there actually is evidence outside the Bible confirming the scriptures, it is usually ignored, discounted as unimportant or denied.

In regard to this passage, suddenly the situation began to change dramatically in favor of the Biblical record. A series of archaeological excavations, some by Albright, discovered a number of buried cities along the route mentioned in Genesis 14.[153] Some of the cities named in Gen. 14, and additional ones, were discovered and even a listing of the very cities from Gen. 14 was uncovered.

It was found that in 2000 B.C. this was a major trade route known as the 'Highway of the Kings.'[154] With all those cities destroyed by the Northern king's invasion, sand had eventually covered them and the trade route.

There was no longer any purpose to travel that area because there were no cities and no people there. It became lost to history until these 20th century A.D. excavations.

At Elba in North Western Syria, also known as Tell Mardikh, a library of 20,000 clay tablets from approximately 2400-2300 B.C. were found. These were written over 900 years before Moses wrote Genesis. One tablet lists the five cities of the plain in the exact sequence as Gen. 14. These documents also show that Genesis correctly reflects the culture of that era, and that the area was flourishing prior to its destruction as recorded in Gen. 14.

Two Elamite kings were also discovered with the same names as two of those in Gen. 14:1. As far as we know, these do not seem to be the same kings, but this definitely proved the names to be historically accurate names of these people and of their rulers prior to 2000 B.C. Chedorlaomer is now a known Elamite name type. Amraphel is known to be a name of both Akkadian and Amorite peoples. Arioch is similar to both Amorite and Horite names. Tidal is a well-documented Hittite name.

Three documents in the British museum refer to several of these kings and that Chedorlaomer formed alliances to put down revolts against his empire. These documents refer to 'Chedorlaomer,' 'Dursirilani, son of Arioch,' 'Tidal and the king of Shinar.' It is also indicated that they later turn against one another.[155]

So, the king's names are all valid historical names from that area and era, and both the names and location of the cities mentioned in Gen. 14 were proven to be actual cities from that time.

Further discoveries showed that 300-400 years before Abraham the Elamites claimed to have control of the area of Palestine and that Sargon I, an Elamite king, had made raids into Syria and Canaan as early as 2300

B.C. So, contrary to previous assumptions, Albright acknowledged travel and conquest was as extensive as Gen. 14 indicated.[156]

It was also confirmed that confederations or alliances of kings did exist before and during the second millennium B.C., but had apparently ceased at some point for unknown reasons and did not exist in the first millennium B.C.

In addition, the second millennium B.C. was the only time the Elamites were aggressively involved in Palestine, validating the early date of these events. As to trade and travel, Babylonian traders were active in Asia Minor (modern Turkey) during Sargon's rule. During the same era, the king of Ugalet (an ancient city in Syria) complained to the king of a city near Ankara, Turkey, of the activities of some of the Hittite traders.

It is also known that Shinar was used by the Egyptians in ancient times to refer to Babylon; that Ellassar is an ancient title for Assyria; that Elim refers to the area that is modern day Iran. Goiim is less certain but because the king's name is Hittite, it is assumed to be the ancient Hittite area in what is today Western Turkey.

So, the first four objections to the historicity of Gen 14 were not only removed, but the historical reliability of those aspects of the passage, were completely substantiated, in great detail. Whoever wrote this had to have had access to firsthand knowledge of the cities, culture, people, practices, and rulers of that time.

But, what about the last objection? How could Abraham and a few hundred men overcome an army that had just defeated an alliance of five kings? Here again archaeology has given us answers.

From archaeological findings, we have learned that armies which had successfully conquered their enemies would have the main army march on ahead with a small rear guard to control the prisoners who herded the animals and carried the other captured goods because this group would move more slowly and gradually become more and more distant from the main army. Also, ancient armies were very much smaller than those of modern times. Hammurabi and his ally king of Mari sent an army of 600 against Elam a major opponent at the time.[157]

In addition, Gen. 14:15, speaking of Abraham, states *"he divided his forces by night."* In other words, Abe attacked from several directions at night. It would have been relatively easy for a small group to overpower these minimal troops – especially when attacking at night since it is impossible to know the size of the attacking forces.

In addition, we don't know the precise size of Abraham's alliance. There is no mention of how many additional men may have been with his three allies. These archaeological findings demonstrated there was now no valid reason for rejecting the statement of Abraham's victory and of the complete historical reliability of this passage. Every element of the record fits the history of the era it purports to relate to, and it does not fit with conditions and practices of any later time.

So, every one of the supposed arguments against the historical validity of Genesis 14 were resolved in favor of the Biblical text. No valid reason remains for rejecting its historical accuracy. The evidence in fact has increased since the initial findings. Another example is the word for 'trained men' in Gen. 14:14. It appears nowhere else in the Old Testament. It is found in Egyptian texts of the 19th century B.C. and once in the 15th century B.C. and apparently disappeared from use after that time.

This suggests that whoever first recorded this account had to have written it while this word was still in use. Someone writing hundreds or more years later would not have known the word and would instead have used a word in current usage at the time they were writing.

Whoever wrote the original account had to have been close enough to the actual events to have known all the relevant information to write so accurately and with all the correct names, including the names of the cities that soon disappeared from history. Because of all these discoveries, there was no longer any excuse to reject the historical validity of this account. Albright himself had made some of these discoveries.

These and additional archaeological discoveries corroborating details in the Old Testament caused Albright to change his mind about the trustworthiness of those writings. In a later book titled <u>History, Archaeology and Christian Humanism</u>, Albright, recounting these and other discoveries, declared that the Old Testament was over all beyond doubt historically accurate and a reliable guide to the past. In another book, he also wrote: *"There can be no doubt that archaeology has confirmed the substantial historicity of Old Testament tradition."* [158]

There have been over 100 thousand archaeological discoveries that relate to the scriptures. For example, Samuel, Kings, and Chronicles list the kings of Israel and 47 Gentile kings of the surrounding nations. Not one of these was known to secular history and so the Bible was ridiculed as mere fiction and myth, however archaeology has confirmed the existence of every one of those kings in the very areas and in the sequence the Bible mentioned.[159]

Millar Burrows, a prominent former Yale University

archaeologist, wrote that not one discovery has ever contradicted a Biblical text. Nelson Glueck, a famous Israeli archaeologist, has declared the same.[160] In fact, Glueck used references in the Old Testament to find Solomon's copper mines which were said to have never existed. They are being mined again today. He also found Solomon's smelting furnaces located at Ezion-geber at the edge of the Gulf of Abaqa. These are the largest smelters that have been found in antiquity.[161]

The following are examples of skeptics' arguments from silence: They formerly claimed that there was no such city as UR, no such people as the Hittites, no significant presence of the Hebrews in Egypt as presented in Exodus, no such pagan kings as listed in Kings and Chronicles, no Jewish king David, no copper mines of Solomon, etc.

Many critical scholars doubted that there was a historical king David despite all the information about him in the Old Testament. They argued that he was a literary creation or myth developed from many heroic traditions to explain the existence of Israel's monarchy. However, in 1993-94 pieces of a stele were found in northern Israel speaking of warfare between Israel and the Arameans. The writing mentions victory over a *"king of Israel of the house of David."*[162] This is dated a little prior to 800 B.C.[163]

All these details including many more that were previously rejected have been confirmed from non-Biblical sources. Truly, this approach of critics has come back to bite them on numerous occasions but they still depend upon it because they often have nothing else.

"Biblical Archaeology in the News Again!"

From Deuteronomy 27:2-4 we learn that the children

of Israel were to set up stone monuments in Mount Ebal when they inherited the land of Canaan and to overlay them with plaster. In the plaster was to be inscribed "very plainly" the words of the law.

"Apparently this passage reflected a custom of monument-making which was frequent in the ancient East, for the text of a similar inscription was discovered in 1967 and reported in the March, 1976 Biblical Archaeologist which bears indirectly upon the story of Balsam as reported in Numbers 22-24.

"The fragmentary text (or possible texts) was found at Tell Deir-'Alla in Jordan by Dr. H.J. Franken. It is written in a dialect of Aramaic which has many affinities with Biblical Hebrew and dates from around 700 B.C. The lines are written in a kind of poetic idiom."
164

The article reporting on this discovery states, *"Here is one of the important aspects of the discovery: Previously, Aramaic poetry dating before the Christian era was unknown. Further, the character of the material is prophetic and this makes it the first prophecy of any scope from the ancient West Semitic world outside the prophecies of the Old Testament."*
165

Here are a couple of important comments from Jacob Hoftijzer as to content of the inscription:

"The first combination contains a prophecy in the name of the prophet Balaam, the son of Beor, known in the Old Testament (Num. 22-24; Deut. 23:5-6; Josh. 13:22; 24:9-10; Neh. 13:2; Mic. 6:5, and see also Num. 31:8 and 16).

"According to Old Testament tradition, this non-Israelite prophet had been summoned by the king of Moab to curse the Israelites, who were marching through Trans-Jordan into Palestine proper; but

through God's Intervention Balaam was obliged to bless the Israelites rather than to curse them.

"In the Old Testament Balaam is clearly a figure who belongs exclusively to traditions about Trans-Jordan, it is noteworthy then, that our texts in which he plays a central role, likewise come from a Trans-Jordanian holy place. Also, in our texts Balaam has no connection whatever with anything that can be considered characteristic of typically Israelite religion.

"If one combines the Biblical data with those of Deir–'Alla, one most conclude that for a considerable period of time the figure of Balaam took up a prominent position in a specific religious tradition In Transjordan." [166]

So, why trust the Old Testament including the book of Genesis? One very significant reason: because it is a historically reliable book. It has been verified over and over including specific details that one would never have expected to be ever able to confirm.

Quoting from Albright, *"Discovery after discovery has established the accuracy of innumerable details, and has brought increased recognition of the Bible as a source of history."* [167] The discoveries of archaeology continue to verify detail after detail in the Old Testament.

How did the authors of the Bible all avoid the mistaken beliefs that were accepted by the surrounding cultures? And how did they know the truth? At the time of Job approximately 2000 B.C., one culture contemporary with Job believed that the earth sat on the back of four giant elephants which stood on the shell of a huge tortoise that swam in a gigantic ocean. Even more recently the Romans believed that the god Atlas carried the earth on his back.

But Job wrote: *"He hangs the earth upon nothing."*

(Job 26:7). So, the Bible avoids the scientific mistakes that were believed at the time of its writing, yet wrote in common observational language so it could be understood throughout the centuries. Another reason for confidence in the Bible is the accurate fulfillment of events predicted often many hundreds and even thousands of years in advance (Gen. 3:15; Deut. 18:15; Psa. 22; Isa. 53; Zach. 12:10; Matt. 24:4, 24).

There are two kinds of Bible critics: those who leap over abundant, reliable evidence with a single bound. They ignore or deny evidence that contradicts their biases or dismiss it with an authoritarian assertion as if their declaration somehow invalidates the evidence.

For these skeptics, no amount of evidence will suffice because the problem is not intellectual or lack of evidence. The issue is their pre-suppositional bias and unwillingness to embrace the truth when it doesn't lead where they want to go. It doesn't matter what God does, they will evade, twist, or deny the evidence. Or as C.S. Lewis once said of these people – whatever God does will be used against Him.

To recap, a major approach of this type of critic is that if nothing is known about a Biblical reference outside of the Bible, the critics assert that it is merely legend and never happened. The absence of information is an excuse to deny the Biblical record. As you may recall, this is called an argument from silence which is no evidence or argument at all. If evidence is found that verifies that scripture, this type of critic either ignores it or claims it is insufficient or invalid or merely moves onto another argument.

The other type of critic though often reluctant, will follow the evidence where it leads and embrace it. Modern examples of this group are former atheists G.K. Chesterton, Cyril Joad, Gerhard Dirks, C.S. Lewis, Josh McDowell, Chuck Colson, Lee Strobel, and many

others.

Part Two

ARCHAEOLOGY AND THE OLD TESTAMENT

The Old Testament, Genesis in particular, is frequently rejected as myth and legend by critics and in media presentations. As a result, most people think there must be discoveries that disprove its authenticity and historicity. There are even occasional claims of discoveries that are used to give the illusion that the Bible and Christian Faith have been disproven.[168]

However, upon scholarly investigation such discoveries claiming to disprove the Bible are always proven to be bogus or based upon false assumptions and misinterpretations. In fact, the truth about the Old Testament is the opposite of what most people seem to think. In the following pages, you will discover additional reasons why the Old Testament is, and should be recognized as reliable history.

Archaeology is a fairly recent discipline. The combination of two Greek words creates the word archaeology. These are the word 'archaios', which means old or ancient, and 'Logos' meaning word, treatise, or study.[169] McDowell gives a brief literal definition of archaeology as *"the study of antiquity."* [170] Archaeology is the study of the past through discovery, analysis and interpretation of the remains of ancient cultures. This includes *"the material remains of human life, thought and activity coordinated with available information concerning the ancient environment."*[171]

Early exploration in Biblical lands was all too often mainly a treasure hunt. People were just looking for rare, unusual, or spectacular items they might collect or sell. Those who engaged in digging often destroyed much of value because there was no established methodology or systematic approach to preserving the contents of these ancient sites.[172]

Near the end of the nineteenth century, methodology began to improve significantly. Flanders Petrie and F.J. Bliss are two who helped to establish a more scientific basis for archaeology in Palestine. They tried very carefully to excavate one layer of habitation at a time to avoid mixing materials from different eras. They also made precise notes of pottery styles and other artifacts found at each layer. Learning the changes in pottery style over time has become one major way of giving approximate dates to each level being excavated.[173]

Today, archaeological teams include members of other sciences and various specialists. These include anthropologists, botanists, epigraphers, geologists, zoologists, and architectural, bone and pottery experts. These various specialists, working together, attempt to reconstruct as closely as possible the site's ancient environment.[174]

Explaining the meaning of a few terms used extensively in archaeology will help the person unacquainted with this field to better understand what they are about to read.

A 'tell' is a mound made up of the remains of several or more different levels of human habitation. Ancient cities tended to be built on high ground which made it easier to defend against attackers. At some point, the city might be abandoned due to its destruction by an earthquake or enemy; or due to an epidemic, drought, or alteration of a trade route.[175]

Later, the reason for its original choice for settlement would draw new inhabitants to rebuild there. The original site would be leveled and then a new city built on top of the older construction. Sometimes materials left from the older habitation would be reused in the new construction. In a particularly good location, this cycle might be repeated many times over the centuries and millennia causing the site to grow higher each time. The Biblical lands have large numbers of these artificially created mounds or hills from ancient times.

Another important term is 'ostraca.' This refers to broken pieces of pottery which ancient peoples had used as a writing material. Since pottery styles changed over time and varied in different cultures, it became a clue to the specific time and culture a piece of pottery had originated. The writings often became further clues as to the particular culture and events of those eras.

A third term that is important to understand is 'stele.' A stele is an upright monument constructed to record some significant event accomplished or claimed by a king or other ruler which is inscribed in stone.

When ancient artifacts from Bible times and locations began to be found in the nineteenth century, the word archaeology was applied to these non-written discoveries. [176] Archaeology in reference to the Old Testament deals with any information that has or may be discovered about humanity prior to the Patriarchs as well as the Patriarchal age itself. It applies as well to the beginnings of Israel as a nation, with its history and with all the interactions between Israel and the nations involved with it.

The modern science of Archaeology has provided spectacular discoveries that confirm many specific details of the Old Testament including even key events of Genesis. In addition, there are other discoveries that indicate the reliability of the cultural events as presented in various passages of the Biblical scriptures. In these cases, the specific Biblical event has not been verified by outside discoveries, but the cultural factors presented in the

Biblical text are appropriate to the time and places the Bible is presenting. That is strong support for the validity of those biblical records

Having accurate cultural elements supports the Bible's reliability, because the writers had to have been familiar with those cultural features. Since cultures differ from one another and are continually changing, the Biblical writings were made near the time of the events presented or those cultural features would not have been accurately presented. That the Old Testament correctly identifies the gods of the pagan nations with which it is interacting at the time, is an example of cultural appropriateness.[177] We will survey both types of these discoveries.

More recently for dating purposes, many archaeologists have begun using B.C.E. meaning Before the Common Era, and C.E. meaning Common Era rather than the previous practice of using B.C. and A.D. This is stated as being used to be a more religiously neutral dating reference since the earlier time designations both related to Jesus' life. Of course, even these new designations are still using time divided by the life of Jesus. Unless quoting materials using B.C.E. I will continue using B.C.

It is also important for readers to realize that the few examples of archaeological finds shared here do not come anywhere near exhausting the examples available. Discoveries that confirm events, names and other details in the Old Testament could be multiplied many hundreds of times beyond what are presented here.

Benefits And Limitations Of Archaeology

Professor Keith Schoville of the University of Wisconsin informs us, *"that despite all the work that scholars do in interpreting the Bible, the only real new*

95

light that we have coming into our study of the Bible is what archaeology provides. So, archaeology and the interface between archaeology and Biblical text is an important consideration for everyone who is a Biblical scholar, whether they be a professor in seminary or a lay person in a Sunday school class."[178]

In addition to confirming details of the Biblical narratives, discoveries of writing in the Biblical and related languages have helped to improve our translations and to clarify the meaning of words that have previously been difficult to understand and translate.[179]

An example of archaeology clarifying the meaning of Hebrew words is in regard to the word 'pim' which occurs in 1 Samuel 13:21, and nowhere else in the Bible. In the King James version, of year 1611, 'pim' was translated 'file.' Archaeology has since found from ancient Israel, several small weights which have the word 'pim' on them. It turns out that 'pim' referred to the charge that the Philistines made for sharpening tools for the people during a time they controlled Israel. It is somewhat less than a shekel.

Modern English translations reflect this new awareness. The 1995 update of the New America Standard version changed the verse to state, "the charge was two-thirds of a shekel ..." [180]

Another example of archaeology clarifying the meaning of a word is that of 'Que,' which occurs in 1 Kings 10:28. The meaning was wrongly guessed in the King James Version as "linen yarn" because there was no place known named Que. The word has since been found to be an ancient reference for Cilicia which was a small state between the Taurus mountains and the Mediterranean Sea in what is now southern Turkey.[181]

The Ugaritic language is named for the ancient city of

96

Ugarit (Modern Ras Shamra) in Syria. This alphabetic language was especially prominent in Syria from 1500 to 1200 B.C.[182] Ugaritic and Biblical Hebrew are very similar. Rare Hebrew words are often more common in Ugaritic which has helped to clarify the meaning of some difficult Old Testament passages. [183] Also, Ugaritic poetry has similarities to Hebrew poetry including parallelisms.[184]

Our knowledge of the chronology of events in the Bible has also been aided by archaeology. The Hebrews dated events from the beginning of a king's reign and began over again from the reign of the next king. They did not create a consecutive dating system. Archaeology has helped to link many Old Testament events to a reasonably accurate time frame.[185]

Another benefit received from archaeology is that many discoveries add further details to events mentioned in the Bible as well as filling in information that occurred in between events recorded in the Biblical accounts. Adding more of the historical context helps with understanding the Bible itself. The Bible does not seek to give a full account of Jewish history and culture, so archaeological details greatly assist our understanding.[186]

"Egyptian reports like 'The Tale of Sinuhe' show how Palestine appeared to Egyptians about the time of Abraham."[187] The Tell Amarna tablets are letters to the Egyptian pharaohs from Palestinian rulers showing the instability in Palestine prior to Israel's invasion. That instability made it easier for Israel to succeed in their invasion and conquests.[188]

Two examples of archaeology adding unknown information about Biblical characters are told on a monument set up by Shalmaneser III, king of Assyria. First, in 853 B.C. king Ahab of Israel participated in a confederation allied against Assyria in the Battle of

Qarqar. Later king Jehu paid tribute to Shalmaneser III. Neither of these events is recorded in the Bible.[189]

Prior to archaeology, the Bible seemed to be a witness to an alien world known as 'sacred history.' It seemed rather foreign, disconnected with the real world and normal life. However, now that apparent separation between the sacred and real world is increasingly dissolved. Through the discoveries of antiquity, the two worlds have been brought together and the Biblical narratives are seen to be part of the genuine history of this world.

Archaeologist Randell Price quotes Gonzalo Baez-Camargo, *"No longer do we see two different worlds, one the world of 'sacred history' and the other the world of 'profane history.' All of history is one history and it is God's history, for God is the God of all history."*[190] Archaeology has succeeded in bringing the two worlds of sacred Biblical history and profane or secular history together as one reality.

Expanding on that insight, Eakins and Lewis state that, *"One of the greatest contributions of archaeology lies in its ability to break down barriers of time and culture and to move the reader of the Bible back into its ancient context providing fresh insight and increased understanding of the scripture."*[191]

After mentioning that modern reliable Bible translations make it easier to enter the world of the Bible, Archaeologist Donald Wiseman added, *"Archaeology also makes it much easier today to enter the world of the Bible. Unfortunately, many people are unaware of the archaeological discoveries and still bring to their consideration of the Bible presuppositions that it may not be authoritative, trustworthy or relevant."*[192]

In other words, many people still have an outdated perspective that assumes there is no valid evidence that the Bible is historically and culturally accurate. This is very unfortunate because the opposite is true; there is extensive evidence the Bible is reliable. It is also unfortunate because the Biblical message is so crucial to all humanity.

It is important not to ignore the valuable contributions of archaeology to our knowledge and confidence in the Biblical text. However, it is just as important not to expect what is impossible for archaeology to accomplish. At this point archaeological excavations involve only a relatively few locations of the thousands of possible sites and even those are mostly only partially excavated. Therefore, much of the information in the Bible may continue to lack external confirmation.

There are limitations to what archaeology can recover or confirm. Professor and Director of Hebrew University's Jerusalem Institute of Archaeology Amihai Mazar refers to these limitations: *"Archaeology is of course limited. Archaeology deals mainly with material culture, not so much with ideas, philosophy, poetry, wisdom etc. as we have in the Bible."*[193]

Professor of History Edwin Yamauchi has gone into specific detail as to the particular reasons for limitations on what archaeology can provide.[194] Randell Price has updated this information.
(1) *"Only a fraction of what is made or written survives."*
(2) *"Only a fraction of available archaeological sites have been surveyed."*
(3) *"Only a fraction of the surveyed sites have been excavated."*[195]
(4) "Only a fraction of an excavation site is actually examined." Egyptologist K.A. Kitchen mentions that typically 95% of a site remains unexcavated, therefore whatever evidence might exist may remain

undetected.[196]

(5) "Only a fraction of what is excavated is eventually reported and published."[197]

Then add to the above list, limitations on the available finances and the lack of qualified personnel necessary to follow up on discoveries made. You can see that there are very severe limitations as to what we can expect archaeology to accomplish.

As you can see from just this listing, most of what has been made and done is no longer available for study; most of what might still be available to us from antiquity may never be discovered and much of what is discovered will never be made known to the public. This greatly limits our prospects of ever confirming most of the information we have in the Bible. Related to those limitations is the problem of preventing theft at archaeological sites.

Protection of sites in the process of being excavated has proven to be very difficult. There are persons who make their living by regularly stealing objects from these sites. Precious objects are looted and often sold on the black market to collectors before the finds are even documented. These items are usually lost to science and their possible significance remains undiscoverable.

It is also important to recognize, as Dewayne Bryant reminds us, that *"Historical texts from any age of human civilization mention a great deal that will be undetectable in the archaeological record, so the historian must use good sense in evaluating the truth claims of his sources. To this effect one must ask two important questions: Does the story fit the available data? And is the story internally consistent?"* [198]

He is saying that in many cases the written records may be all we ever have available, so these must be carefully but fairly evaluated. He also states that we

100

must compare the written documents, both Biblical scripture and those other writings discovered, with any related other artifacts that archaeology uncovers, but that artifacts will never be able to verify everything found in the writings of antiquity.

These very significant limitations upon the results of archaeology do however make even more amazing the number of archaeological discoveries that have already confirmed Biblical records of events, rulers, other persons, and the cultural appropriateness of much information in the Biblical documents.

Another aspect of the importance of archeology is pointed out by the Director of the Hebrew University's Institute of Archaeology in Jerusalem. Amihai Mazar made the important observation that, *"archaeology is our only source of information that comes directly from the Biblical period itself ... Archaeology can give us information right away from the period when things happened ..."*[199] The artifacts excavated from ancient times take us back to the situations where those items were part of human life and experience.

The artifacts and information uncovered by archaeology involve historical, geographical, and cultural facts. Biblical archaeology cannot prove the Bible to be God's word, but it can verify that the people, their culture, and events recorded in the Biblical narratives are authentic history. Archaeology has frequently provided clarification and verification of the Biblical text.

Archaeology has revealed some great distinctions between secular historians and the Biblical records. For example, though the Greek and Arab historians are consistently inaccurate and unreliable when referring to the kings of Egypt, Assyria and Babylon, the Biblical narratives have been proven to be exact and trustworthy.[200] To account for this accuracy from a human perspective, requires that the writers were contemporaries or had access to accurate original documents. Such accuracy, also makes it certain that the copyists were very careful to reliably pass on the text they had received.[201]

When such validation of the Biblical narratives does occur, that fact, does justify consideration of the claims of the Bible to be from God. Validation of the ancient Biblical text would seem to require an honest examination and evaluation of any additional available evidence of divine origin as well.

Another of those evidences of the Divine origin of the Old Testament is its uniqueness when considered in the light of other ancient Near Eastern religious literature. As Price points out, *"The discoveries of the religious literature of the Sumerians, Egyptians, Hittites, Assyrians, Babylonians and Canaanites have all highlighted the originality and elevated morality of the Bible. Therefore, archaeology is able to offer confirmation of Biblical revelation by discrediting historical skepticism and, at the same time, demonstrating Scriptures theological distinctiveness."* [202] What could be the source or origin of this uniqueness?

Yale Archaeologist Miller Burrows mentions, *"Archaeology has in many cases refuted the views of modern critics. It has shown in a number of instances that those views rest on false assumptions and unreal, artificial schemes of historical development (AS1938 p. 182). This is a real contribution, and not to be minimized."* [203] Modern critics do, however seek to minimize and deny the value of such discoveries of archaeology.

The great archaeologist W.F. Albright agreed with Burrows. *"The excessive skepticism shown toward the Bible by important historical schools of the* eighteenth and nineteenth centuries, certain phases of which still appear periodically, has been progressively discredited. Discovery after discovery has established the accuracy of innumerable details and has brought increased recognition to the value of the Bible as a source of history." [204] Albright was originally one of those skeptics who however allowed the evidence to alter his perspective!

Burrows also wrote that, "The excessive skepticism of many liberal theologians stems not from a careful evaluation of the available data, but from an enormous predisposition against the supernatural." [205] Burrows has stated that it is the anti-supernatural bias of the critic that is the actual basis for their rejection of the validity of the Biblical narratives.

Former professor Raymond Bowman of the University of Chicago noted that, "The confirmation of the Biblical narrative at most points has led to a new respect for Biblical tradition and a more conservative conception of Biblical history." [206]

Peter Farb, a Fellow of the American Association for the Advancement of Science, wrote about Dr. Nelson Glueck, one of the world's most respected archaeologists. In regard to Gleuck' discoveries, Farb stated, "To him the Bible is an indispensable tool for seeking out lost cities, caravan routes, and details of the everyday life of Biblical times. His amazing number of important archaeological discoveries is due largely to the faith he places in the Bible's accuracy about the land and its peoples." [207]

Farb stated that Gleuck just basically used the Hebrew Scriptures and an Arab guide to make his phenomenal discoveries. Gleuck, himself has stated that, "Scores of archaeological findings have been made which confirm in clear outline or in exact detail historical statements in the Bible." [208]

Farb continued that, *"Through his careful study, Dr. Glueck has been able to locate more than fifteen hundred ancient sites. He has helped to trace much of Abraham's route to the Promised Land and to date approximately when the exodus of the Israelites from Egypt took place. Bible in hand, he located the long-lost mines of Solomon at Ezion-geber and discovered the seaport to which Solomon's fleet brought ivory, apes and peacocks. Dr Glueck and his tireless co-workers have made the mute rocks of the Holy Land speak."*[209]

In a lecture at Temple Immanuel, Dallas, Texas, Dr. Gleuck complained that he was being labeled a fundamentalist because of his statements about archaeology confirming the Bible. He said, *"I have been accused of teaching the verbal plenary inspiration of the scripture. I want it to be understood that I have never taught this. All I have ever said is that in all my archaeological investigation I have never found one artifact of antiquity that contradicts any statement of the word of God."*[210]

Creation

Though there were no humans around to witness the creation, there have been numerous creation accounts discovered from various cultures all over the world. The Babylonian account, called the <u>Atrahasis Epic,</u> is from the seventh century B.C. though it probably originated earlier. The <u>Enuma Elish</u> presents creation from the Babylonian and Assyrian religious perspectives. Despite the gross mythology and polytheism, these two accounts both have some parallels with the Genesis account. [211]

A more recent discovery is a creation account at Ebla in northern Syria. Made prior to 2000 B.C. the account reads, *"Lord of heaven and earth:/ The earth was not, you created it;/ The light of day was not, you created*

104

it."[212] This account appears to have been written prior to the additions and distortions of later mythology.

How are we to explain these parallels with the Biblical account? The critics either dismiss all such accounts as legend and myth, or declare the Genesis account to be a sanitized or cleaned up version of the creation myth, since the Biblical writing is much more recent. These dismissive arguments are however unverifiable assumptions lacking in evidence.

Robert Dick Wilson wrote that *"there is sufficient resemblance between them [the various accounts] to point to a common origin antedating the time of Abraham's departure from Ur of the Chaldees."*[213]

The claim that the Genesis creation account was borrowed from the earlier accounts is dealt with by Alan Millard who coauthored a book on the <u>Atrahasis Epic</u>. *"All who suspect or suggest borrowing by the Hebrews are compelled to admit large-scale revision, alteration and reinterpretation in a fashion that cannot be substantiated for any other composition from the ancient Near East or in any other Hebrew writing ..."*[214]

Rather than a revision of an earlier pagan account, it is more likely that the Biblical account is from the original account passed down without the contamination and distortions of later pagan mythology. The Biblical explanation of creation in Genesis is consistent with Israel's unique monotheistic and non-mythological theology.[215] As to the late date of Moses writings, in comparison with earlier creation accounts, he may have received this original account from older uncontaminated documents from the time of Abraham or even earlier.

The Genesis record may also have been accurately passed down orally prior to that. We do not know whether God preserved a very early accurate record of the beginning or whether God revealed this information directly to Moses.

On an ancient cylinder seal is *"a seated woman reaching for one of two fruits hanging from a tree. A man also reaches for the fruit opposite her, and behind her a serpent slithers. It has every key element from the Fall on man found in Genesis 3."*[216] This is confirming evidence that other early cultures knew of the story of the temptation and Fall of humanity. This should be seen as a confirmation of the Biblical record.

The Genesis Flood

There are about two hundred or more different flood legends from cultures all around the earth. Though there are many variations in the details given in the various stories, there are also central recurring themes in most of them. These recurring central themes are quite reflective of the account given in Genesis 6-8. The accounts from Middle Eastern cultures tend to be the most similar to the Biblical account.[217]

Critics deny the global flood presented in Genesis assuming this is an exaggeration and expansion of memories of a serious local flood several millennia ago. It is more difficult to account for the virtually universal reports of a flood destroying nearly all of humanity. Critics assume that something in humanity's psyche causes each culture to create similar myths and legends regarding ancient events. That is a convenient but unverifiable assumption.

These kinds of arguments by critics are used to devalue and dismiss evidence when it does support the Bible. When there is no evidence either way regarding information in the Bible, the critic charges that the Bible is in error and unreliable. When there is supportive evidence, it is often dismissed as an example of natural tendencies in humans that create widespread mythological beliefs. So, when there is no information that absence is used against the Bible. However, actual evidence is also distorted in such a way as to appear not to be evidence. These kinds of methods are the basis of most criticisms of the Bible.

According to William W. Hallo, curator of the Yale University Babylonian artifacts collection, there are references in Sumerian cuneiform literature at about 2600 B.C. to antediluvian (pre-flood) cities that may correspond to two such cities mentioned in Genesis 4:17-18.[218]

The fundamental issue behind the critical attack on the flood is that it has the intervention of God into human history and indicates judgment upon human evil. These supernatural features contradict the critic's worldview and result in denial of the event and the evidence for it.

It is more credible to accept the similarity of the global flood stories as resulting from a real historical event which was remembered and passed down to the descendants of the survivors of the event. Variations in the different flood accounts are due to the specifics of a culture's theology and the role of mythology or lack thereof in that culture.[219]

The Patriarchs

Both liberal Jewish and liberal Gentile scholars frequently deny the historicity of the Patriarchs. The claim is that Abraham never lived and that the Biblical stories of the patriarchs were legends that were projected back into ancient history by nationalistic Jews in the middle of the first millennium (600-400 B.C.). [220] These are, however, claims based upon disbelief in the reliability of the Old Testament; assumptions justified due to the lack of any information outside the Bible specifically naming any of the patriarchs. There is no objective evidence to support the skeptic's claims.

Remember that earlier the critics made similar claims, confidently asserting that the Hittites never existed. The critics were proven wrong! The Hittite civilization including its capitol and a large library was found in Western Turkey. [221] It is significant that Biblical references to the Hittites are scattered among the accounts of the patriarchs and later. Those references to the historical Hittites among patriarchal accounts support that the records regarding the patriarchs are also historical.[222]

W.F. Albright had written in regard to the reliability of the patriarchal tradition of Genesis that *"Numerous recent excavations in sites of this period in Palestine, supplemented by finds made in Egypt and Syria, give us a remarkably precise idea of patriarchal Palestine, fitting well into the picture handed down in Genesis."*[223]

He also wrote, *"This has been strikingly confirmed by the linguistic data found in recently excavated inscriptions. Genesis derives the ancestors of Israel from Mesopotamia – archaeological evidence agrees."*[224]

Albright has informed us that despite skeptical and liberal theological claims, there are solid reasons for accepting the stories of the patriarchs as historically valid. For example, excavations have shown that the names in the Hebrew genealogies of Genesis are similar to those in the surrounding cultures of those times.[225]

According to the critics, Ur was a fictional city of legend. It has been found much to their chagrin. Albright goes on to state that *"excavations have proved that Ur was at the height of its prosperity from about 2060 to about 1950 B.C. ... when it was destroyed by invading Elamites. Ur was partially restored ... in the early seventeenth century it was destroyed and disappears from history for centuries."*[226]

It was doubted among critical scholars whether Haran had ever existed. Archaeology has confirmed it to have been in existence four thousand years ago, probably as part of the kingdom of Mari in southeastern Turkey.[227]

We do not have precise dates as yet for Abraham, however the descriptions of Haran and Palestine[228] as well as cultural details of his dealings with the Hittites fits best around 1900 B.C. We also do know that Haran and Nahor were flourishing cities in the nineteenth and eighteenth centuries B.C. (Genesis 11:31; 24:10).[229]

Quoting Albright again, *"Furthermore, all the places with which Abraham is connected in Syria and Palestine can be shown to have been important caravan stations; for most of them there is archaeological or documentary evidence of occupation in the nineteenth-eighteenth centuries B.C."* [230]

Genesis mentioned Abraham and Isaac having dug wells in the arid Negeb desert (Genesis 21:30; 26:18-32). Archaeologists have searched in that area and found the wells and the pure water that had not been known of for thousands of years.[231] That is another detail proving the reliability of Genesis. Genesis also mentions that Abraham planted a Tamarisk tree in Beersheba (21:33). Forestry experts tried doing the same and found that those trees flourished in that area despite the very low rainfall there.[232]

It has been questioned how Abraham could have traversed the Negeb with his livestock. Today the

Negeb desert is one of the harshest on earth. Archaeology has discovered that in Abraham's era the Negeb was very different than in modern times. It was then dotted with oases, agricultural land, and settlements close enough for travel between them without running out of water. [233] The region was sparsely populated which would also have allowed for large herds and flocks to traverse the land.

Genesis mentions Abraham's heir as one of his servants (Gen. 15:1-6), then later that Sarah had a son by proxy through her Egyptian maid, Hagar. At the ancient city of Nuzi, clay tablets were discovered revealing that both of these were long followed practices among couples who could not have children. It was expected of a barren wife that she arrange for a slave girl to have a child by her husband.[234]

This child by proxy became the heir unless the true wife later had a natural child. There were specific laws protecting the rights of each of the persons involved.[235] The slave girl was assured of economic security. [236] This indicates the passage is culturally appropriate for the time of Abraham.

Another element of the account of Abraham that was frequently attacked was the mention of camels in Egypt in Genesis chapter 12. The Egyptologist A. Erman, R.H. Pfeiffer, and A.H. Sayce all declared that camels were not introduced into Egypt until centuries after Abraham.[237] The camel was native originally to Arabia and the Euphrates area. Peter Farb mentions that most scholars assume the word for camels was mistakenly added later by a transcriber of the Hebrew text.[238]

However, archaeologist Joseph P. Free gathered conclusive evidence the camel was known in Egypt long before Abraham lived. [239] One example is a camel's skull discovered in Fayum, Egypt, that may date to the time of Abraham. Another is a camel's hair rope discovered that dates to approximately 2500 B.C.

That is about five hundred years before Abraham is thought to have entered Egypt. Also dated about 3000 B.C. are three excavated pottery camel heads and several other artifacts that indicate this early existence of camels in Egypt. [240] Apparently the domestication of camels was still quite rare at those early dates, but it was not unknown as critics claimed.[241]

The covenant between God and Abram in Genesis 15 seems strange to modern man. However, 18th century B.C. clay tablets found in Mari inform us of a ceremony for sealing an agreement or covenant at that time. The sealing of the agreement involved cutting a donkey in half and those committing to the covenant walking between the halves of the donkey.[242] Archaeology shows this was not a fictional story and helps us understand the cultural aspects of the Genesis 15 passage.

As of yet we have found no mention of the Patriarchs outside of the Bible. However, there are reasons to accept the genuineness of their existence as historical persons. These include the proven accuracy of historical and cultural details in the Biblical accounts of the Patriarchs; the ancient tombs at Hebron, alleged to be of the Patriarchs and of their families at Ephrah;[243] the rediscovered wells said to have been dug by Abraham and Isaac; along with the knowledge that the names given in the narratives are appropriate for those time periods.

These facts all attest to the existence of the Patriarchs. [244] An example of the cultural appropriateness of the accounts exists on one of the clay tablets found at Nuzi (in Iraq). These show obvious parallels to the culture and customs of the

Patriarchs including a similar story of a birthright exchange as occurred between Esau and Jacob (Gen. 25:29-34). [245] One of the Nuzi tablets records a birthright being exchanged for three sheep.[246]

Another custom confirmed by the Nuzi tablets is that of Rachel stealing her father's household gods. She and Leah stated: *"Is there any portion or inheritance left for us in our father's house?"* (Gen. 31:14-15). Then Rachel steals the idols from her father (Gen. 31:19). The Nuzi tablets inform us that the household gods were not only idols, but were also associated with rights of inheritance. So, Rachel was taking matters into her own hands.[247]

Despite widespread skepticism regarding the existence of the Patriarchs, the evidence gives us every reason to believe the narratives of Genesis 12-50 are actual history. Also, "no evidence contravenes the trustworthiness of the patriarchal record."[248]

Sodom And Gomorrah

There are a variety of opinions regarding Sodom and Gomorrah among critics and Biblical scholars. Their views vary from those who consider it a complete myth, to others assuming it contains a fragment of historical truth to which imagination was added. Some think the story to be primitive memories of an ancient geological disaster. Of those who have believed this to be a geological disaster, some explain the destruction portrayed in Genesis to be the consequence of a massive earthquake which ignited the bitumen or asphalt that seeped from underground. Two geologists think this occurred around 2350 B.C.[249]

We have every reason to accept that the writer of the account in Genesis 19, believed it to be actual history. There are ancient non-Biblical historians who wrote of this as a real event including some declaring the evidence of the destruction was still evident when they wrote.[250] The Bible specifies in Genesis 14:3 that Sodom and Gomorrah were located in *"the Valley of Siddim (that is the Salt Sea)."* Those are recognized references to the Dead Sea area. This area has been noted for frequent earthquakes and an abundance of asphalt, oil, and natural gas.

Many efforts to find these cities have been unsuccessful. However, Albright discovered a city in the region known in Arabic as Bab edh-Dhray. The city had evidences of having been heavily fortified and possessing a large population. Albright dated this city 3150-2200 B.C. The city's destruction was estimated at approximately 2200 B.C.[251]

The city has been excavated since the mid-1960's, revealing a Canaanite temple and huge cemetery as well as extensive evidence of destruction by fire.[252] The city and cemetery were both covered by a several foot-thick layer of ash and the intense heat had turned mud bricks red.

Archaeologist Bryant Wood discussed the unusual phenomenon at this city's cemetery with Randell Price. During the final phase of this cemetery's use, in contrast to earlier burial, bodies were placed in buildings above ground. Such buildings for the dead are designated as charnel houses by archaeologists. The excavations found that the fire at each charnel house had begun on the roof and then once the roof collapsed burned the building from the inside.[253]

This is not how a fire would naturally spread from building to building. The cemetery and city had the same ash deposits and had been destroyed at the same time. The finding also seemed strange because the cemetery was at such a distance from the town, so the fire would not have spread from one to the other.[254] The evidence seems to indicate this to be the site of Sodom and evidence of the judgment of God pouring fire and brimstone down upon it.

Continued searching discovered there were five more cities in proximity to Bab edh-Dhra along the eastern edge of the Dead Sea. The excavation of these cities reveals that four of them were destroyed at or about the same time. Each of the four indicate the exact same cause of its demise by a huge conflagration. The deep ash deposits at each site have apparently caused the soil to have a spongy charcoal consistency making them unsuitable for resettlement.

The fifth city was spared the disaster but abandoned about the same time, apparently due to the region's destruction. [255] This is Zoar as indicated in other ancient writings and maps. [256] In Genesis 19:19-23 Abraham's nephew Lot requests permission to escape to Zoar, one of the five cities in the area and his request was granted. So, this one city of the five was spared destruction.

A possible explanation as to how this destruction occurred is that given by John D. Morris. *"These five cities had all been situated along the Dead Sea Rift, a major plate boundary. At God's command, the rift ruptured spewing great quantities of liquid and gaseous hydrocarbons high into the atmosphere. These ignited setting the whole region ablaze and covering it with 'fire and brimstone.'"*[257]

The date indicated for this destruction of the 'cities of the plain' (2450-2350 B.C.) is earlier than the assumed presence of Abraham in the region. But we could be wrong (late) in our estimate for the date of Abraham's entry into the land or for how early the destruction occurred. The answer might be a combination of these two possibilities. The archaeological data of the events does agree with the Genesis account, so it

114

seems that these must be the correct locations of Sodom, Gomorrah and the three lesser cities.

The Elba tablets discovered in northern Syria date between 2,400 to 2,250 B.C. Those tablets refer to both Sodom and Gomorrah thus removing all doubt about the existence of those cities. Again, the biblical documents have been validated.[258]

It is said by some critics that there was never a significant presence of Israelites in Egypt in the middle of the second millennium B.C. or before. However, at Beni-hasan in central Egypt, a tomb painting portrays a Semitic caravan of immigrants being presented to a ruler in their multicolored robes.[259] Also some remains of the typical Israelite four room house have been found in the area of Egypt, where the Israelites were said to have lived.

Eckart Frahm, writing in the May/June 2016 issue of Biblical Archaeology Review notes several similarities between the story of Joseph in the later chapters of Genesis and the life of Assyrian king Esarhaddon. He then writes, "*Even though there is no proof, these parallels suggest that the author(s) of the Joseph story borrowed a number of key motifs from the story of Esarhaddon's rise to power. What remains unclear is at what time this borrowing occurred: in the immediate aftermath of Esarhaddon's reign or much later. Both timeframes are feasible.*"[260]

Actually, neither timeframe is at all possible. As Frahm later admits part of the account of Joseph "*does seem to have a genuinely Egyptian background.*"[261] This is a significant admission because the account should have a more Assyrian background, if that were its actual source, especially if it were really written in the sixth century as he presumes.

There are several other problems with Frahm's reasoning. First, Frahm admits there is no proof, but then goes on to assume his conjectures are true; he assumes the borrowing did occur. The bigger problem is that the account of Joseph in Genesis was written prior to 1400 B.C. In addition, there may have been earlier oral transmission and almost certainly earlier written accounts prior to the Genesis narrative regarding Joseph's rise to authority in Egypt.[262]

In attempting to make a comparison between the two stories, we find that Esarhaddon reigned during the golden age in Assyria, from 681 to 669 B.C. It is therefore impossible for the story of Joseph to have been borrowed from a ruler at least eight centuries too late!

According to Genesis 41:14 Joseph was shaved and dressed in new clothes after being brought from prison as preparation to meet with Pharaoh. This is contrary to Semitic practice, but in keeping with Egyptian requirements. Egyptians shaved unless they were in mourning, whereas Semites ordinarily did not shave.[263]

Genesis gives correct Egyptian titles for those used in regard to Joseph's life including *"overseer"*, *"chief butler"*, *"chief baker."* [264] Later Joseph informs his brothers of his Egyptian titles as, *"Father to Pharaoh, Lord of his household and ruler of all Egypt"* (Gen. 45:8). The first title in Egyptian would have been *"father to the gods"* but Joseph made it accord with Hebrew theology as he could not acknowledge any god but Yahweh being genuine. Neither could he acknowledge Pharaoh as a god.

The other two titles he gives are accurate translations of known Egyptian titles.[265] Pharaoh was thought by Egyptians to be the incarnation of the god Horus. Father to the gods or Father to Pharaoh therefore meant that Joseph was Pharaoh's adviser.[266]

Also, the name given by Pharaoh to Joseph is

116

Zaphnath Paaneah (Gen. 41:44). This is an Egyptian title that has been translated in many different ways. It may mean *"one who discovers hidden things,"* *"revealer of secrets,"* *"preserver of life,"* or even *"the god speaks, he lives."* This last translation could relate to the Egyptian belief that the ruling pharaoh was an incarnation of their god, Horus. Pharaoh may have assumed Joseph to be an incarnation of another god for Joseph to have had such insight.

We know when Esarhaddon was alive and that he ruled the Assyrian empire from 681 to 669 B.C.[267] Since we have firm dates for the history of Esarhaddon, the critic must adjust the dates for the Biblical writings in order to justify rejecting the historical validity of the Biblical narratives. Frahm, in keeping with liberal theological bias, is creating the illusion that the later story was the source of the earlier records. This is a recurring strategy.

The critics must assume very late dates for the Biblical writings in order to justify their claims that the Biblical stories are copied from later secular sources rather than being genuine history.

The papyrus D'Orbiney, from about 1185 B.C. tells of the Egyptian "Tale of Two Brothers." These two brothers are living together in one house. The wife of one fails in her attempts to seduce the other and then accuses him of sexually attacking her. The husband expels his brother from the home, later finding his wife had lied and kills her. This part of the story is presented as a comparison of the Genesis account of Potiphar's wife falsely accusing Joseph with her husband placing Joseph in prison.[268]

It again is assumed by Frahm that this part of the Joseph narrative has probably been derived from the Egyptian tale. Aside from the significant variations in two stories, Frahm's assumption is completely invalid as Joseph lived more than 500 years prior to the Egyptian tale.

Frahm also recounts a fifth century B.C. Assyrian story of an advisor to Sennacherib and Esarhaddon who is betrayed by his adopted son and falsely imprisoned. He is to be executed, but reminds the executioner of a favor he had done that had saved that executioner from an unjust death. The executioner kills another prisoner instead of the former advisor and deceives Esarhaddon. Later versions of this story have the advisor helping the Egyptian king and returning triumphantly to Assyria.

Each of these implied sources for the Genesis story of Joseph, were written too late. Also, the differences in the stories are at least as important as the similarities. Frahm is attempting to build a case for the fabrication of the story in Genesis by finding little fragments of comparison from many different sources. There are bound to be some similarities in various stories from different times and cultures because human nature is the same worldwide.

Since these other writings are much later than Joseph's lifetime, it would be more reasonable to consider that perhaps other authors heard about Joseph's life including his amazing rise to authority and drew some ideas for their own stories from his.

Frahm includes a photo of "the Famine Stele" discovered on Sehel Island of the upper Nile in Egypt near Aswan. The inscription on the stele is said to date from 332-331 B.C., [269] but describes a seven-year famine from over 2,000 years prior. There are parallels to the actual event in Genesis 41, but presented from the perspective of Egyptian mythology and polytheism.[270]

Frahm again assumes the Biblical story is based upon this Egyptian story. The lateness of this record as the

118

Egyptian version is reason enough to discount it being the source of the famine element in the Genesis narrative. It is over one thousand years too late to be the origin. It makes more sense to assume that the event recorded in Genesis is the source of this much later Egyptian version of the story.

Egypt And Exodus

Foreign invaders ruled Egypt for the first time in history from about 1700 to 1540 B.C.[271] These Semitic conquers were called Hyksos by the Egyptians. The Hyksos established their capital at Avaris, in northern Egypt. The story of Joseph's rise to power in Egypt fits well with this period of the Hyksos rule. It is believed that since they themselves were foreigners, they were more tolerant of immigrants than native Egyptian rulers. During Hyksos' rule there was unusually high immigration both into and out of Egypt.[272]

The area of Goshen on the Nile delta, where the Hebrews were allowed to settle, was very near the Hyksos capital at Avaris.[273] When the Hyksos were expelled, it is likely the native Egyptian rulers turned against the Hebrews whom the Hyksos had seemingly favored.[274]

The NOVA television documentary titled: "The Bible's Buried Secrets" repeats the skeptical view that Israel's monotheism was the result of a long evolutionary process that finally developed from the experience of exile. This is *"the commonly held view that monotheism was purely a late Israelite invention."*[275] This common explanation appears to answer the question of the origin of monotheism, but it is difficult to validate without ignoring or completely distorting the Biblical narratives as well as what we discover from history and anthropology.

Scripture clearly indicates that the Hebrew religion was monotheistic from its origin. Evidence is very evident from scripture, as well as from archaeology, that many Israelites adopted idolatry and polytheism despite God's commands to the contrary. The prophets were continually reminding and warning the people and rulers of Israel to forsake their idolatry and return to Yahweh. There were occasional temporary returns to monotheism, primarily in Judah, but these restorations were usually short-lived.

The reality of this frequent flirtation with the polytheism of the neighboring nations however is no excuse for critics to ignore the underlying teaching and assumption right from Israel's beginning that there was only one true God. Israel's repeated apostasy is given as the reason for their exile which did finally cure them of idolatry. The exile was not however the origin of monotheism, but it was the cause of a full restoration of commitment to that original teaching of the Old Testament.[276]

An interesting question to contemplate is that, if God did not reveal Himself to Moses and the Israelites, how did they adopt monotheism and the high morality given in Exodus? Another difficult issue would be, what then could be the source of Moses monotheism?

Moses was educated in Egypt whose religion was polytheistic. The nations which the Israelites encountered during their escape from Egypt and the surrounding nations in Canaan were all idol worshippers and polytheistic. Despite these influences and realities, Moses' writings taught that there was only one true God.

It has often been declared by modern scholars that the names of the midwives Shiphrah and Puah in Exodus 1:15 were not authentic. This is due to their assumption that Exodus was written hundreds of years later than the events recorded there. Both names have been found among Northwestern Semites as women's names, one in the eighteenth and the other in the fourteenth century B.C.[277]

This verifies that Exodus, written in the mid-fifteenth century gave appropriate women's names for that era. Had Exodus been written hundreds of years later, as the critics claim, the names of the mid-wives would not have been appropriate for this earlier time.

Eckart Frahm seeks to explain the story of Moses birth and survival in Exodus 2 as originating from the birth "Legend of King Sargon of Akkad." This Sargon founded and ruled the Akkadian empire, ruling from 2334-2279 B.C. Though he was an actual historical person, the account, supposedly his autobiography, was actually written long after his death.[278] The article on Sargon quotes scholar O.A. Gurney explaining this legend to be an example of Mesopotamian naru literature.

"A naru was an engraved stele on which a king would record the events of his reign ... The so-called 'naru literature' consists of a small group of apocryphal naru-inscriptions, composed probably in the early second millennium B. C., but in the name of famous kings of a bygone age. A well-known example is the Legend of Sargon of Akkad. In these works the form of the naru is retained, but the matter is legendary or even fictitious."[279]

If the story of Sargon does predate Moses, his parents could possibly have known of this ancient story of a baby being put into a basket protected against water seeping in and placed in the river. If so, they decided to try it in a serious real-life situation in an effort to save their infant son from being murdered. On the other hand, the Legend of Sargon, was most likely to have been written much later than that of Moses, according to our earliest knowledge of it.

Peter Farb wrote in <u>The Land, Wildlife and Peoples of the Bible</u> that 'Habiru' were engaged in dragging stones for Pharoah's building projects according to Egyptian texts. [280] Thus, the enslavement of the Hebrews in Egypt is verified by Egyptian sources in addition to the record in the Bible.

The Exodus

Archaeologist Bryant Wood, in reaction to skeptical rejection of the Exodus wrote, *"Rather than blindly accept a learned scholars' argument from silence to dismiss the factuality of the Exodus, let us look at the reality of the situation."* [281]

The Exodus has been described as both *"the most significant event in all of the Old Testament"*[282] and *"the Exodus deliverance is depicted as the act by which Israel was brought into being as a people and thus as the beginning point in Israel's history ..."*[283] The Exodus is *"the great saving act of God to which all later generations looked back with thankfulness. It was a miraculous intervention by God in response to the cries of His people (Ex. 3:7)."*[284]

The plagues of deliverance for the Israelites are presented in the book of Exodus as a great victory over and judgment on the many fictional gods of Egypt. This endnote gives a few examples of the inability of the Egyptian gods to protect Egypt or its people from the power of the true living God.[285] This defeat of Egypt's polytheism could have and should have served as a wakeup to Egyptians as to who was truly God.

As yet, archaeology cannot establish the date of the Exodus with any certainty. The early date in the mid 1400's seems to fit Biblical chronology better, but the later date around approximately 1270 B.C. seems to fit better with current archaeological knowledge and interpretation. The later date then creates problems with the timing and events of the conquest of Canaan under Joshua. In addition, some of the data appears to fit well into either the early or later date.

The annual Jewish celebration of Passover has been celebrated for approximately 3,500 years. Passover commemorates the Exodus as God's deliverance of their ancestors from slavery and death in Egypt and the formation of Israel as a unique people and nation.

The theological and historic centrality of the Exodus in Judaism would seem to indicate an original connection with actual past events. It is very unlikely for the record to have included the humiliation of slavery and their rebelliousness against God and Moses, if the story were fictional.[286]

Archaeology has proven the falseness of the movie portrait of an eighty-year-old Moses carrying huge, heavy stone slabs containing the Ten Commandments down rugged mountain terrain. The discovery of similarly inscribed stone slabs have shown that the Ten Commandments were probably inscribed on very thin slices of stone not much larger than a man's hand. This would have been also necessary due to the relatively small size of the ark in which they were deposited along with the later deposit of the original scrolls of the Pentateuch.[287]

The reason why these items were placed in the ark is also clarified by archaeology. During Moses time Near Eastern cultures put legal documents as well as agreements between rival nations in their temples "at the feet of" their main god.[288] This god was to be guardian and supervisor of the implementation of these documents and agreements.

An example of this practice comes from Egyptian records. The treaty between the Hittite king Hattusilis

III and Ramses II was completed by depositing a copy at the feet of Pharaoh's god Ra and that of the Hittites god Teshup. The ark as the footstool of Yahweh meant the tablets of the law of God and scrolls of the Pentateuch were at His feet in the Tabernacle.[289]

It has been common in recent years for critical scholars to declare that there was no presence of Israel in Egypt, no Exodus, no conquest, and that the early Israelites were actually native Canaanites. Mainstream thinking prefers the perspective that the Israelites were Canaanites who had developed a distinct culture that varied from that of the other Canaanites around them. [290] This is unacceptable because of specific cultural evidence as you will see.

It is sometimes suggested that perhaps a small group of Canaanite slaves fled from Egypt which eventually grew until it developed into the story of the Exodus.[291] Such a perspective ignores not merely the Biblical accounts but relevant historical and cultural factors as well.

Despite the celebration of the Exodus since ancient times, the historicity of the event is disputed by critics for a variety of reasons. Two major causes for dispute are that the accounts refer to God and to miraculous plagues visited upon Egypt in order to force Pharaoh to release the Hebrew slaves. These references to the supernatural violate many critics worldview assumptions which leads them to reject the historical reliability of any Biblical writing that includes such information.

Other reasons critics reject the veracity of the Exodus narrative include: (1) Their claim that corroborating evidence has not been found in Egypt or the Sinai; (2) Their claims the accounts were written centuries after the alleged events and are shaped by theological and ideological considerations rather than by history; (3)

124

Their claims the narratives are a mix of myth, legend and folklore.[292] Another reason that some reject the Exodus account is that it would assist in establishing Israel's right to the land.

Egyptologist and archaeologist James Hoffmeier wrote that part of the difficulty is that critics are unreasonable to the extreme in what they require to be sufficient evidence for the historicity of the Exodus.[293] They also ignore or discount the value of the evidence available from Egyptian sources.[294]

The claim is that there is no corroborating evidence in Egypt of the Israelite presence nor of the Exodus. There has been less excavation in the area the Hebrews were said to inhabit, than in other areas of Egypt. This is due to the high-water table which makes excavations more costly as well as there being less likelihood of information surviving that environment. In fact, the Nile delta area is said to not have provided documents from any era of Egyptian History.

In addition, there actually is some Egyptian information available, but minimalist (critical) scholars tend to ignore it. For example, a wall at a tomb in Beni Hassan 200 miles south of Avaris portrays bearded Semites arriving in Egypt with their families and livestock. This portrayal dates about 1900 B.C. These people are called the Amu, the people of God. This was a term used to refer to the ancient Hebrews.[295]

The details of Egyptian court life in Genesis and Exodus along with the use of words showing Egyptian influence in the description of these events reveals a firsthand knowledge of that aspect of Egyptian culture.[296] This would not be possible if someone were writing hundreds of years later from Canaan creating a fictional account.

Quoting Randel Price who refers to specific ancient

documents, *"We have evidence that foreigners from Canaan entering Egypt, lived there, were sometimes considered troublemakers, and that Egypt oppressed and enslaved a vast foreign workforce during several dynasties. We also have records that slaves escaped, and that Egypt suffered from plague-like conditions."*[297]

Price continued, *"We can prove the presence of a people like the Israelites in the Sinai Peninsula, at Kadesh-barnea, and at other places mentioned in the books of the Bible that record this history... Finally, we can provide archaeological data to support several dates for the Conquest and settlement periods, which followed the Exodus. This data comes from such sites as Jericho, Megiddo, and Hazor."*[298]

Egyptologist Manfred Beitak's article "Israelites Found In Egypt" verifies Israel's presence in Egypt over 3000 years ago through the discovery of the typical Hebrew construction of workers' huts where the Hebrews had settled in Egypt. The article also indicates that the geography presented in the book of Exodus shows intimate knowledge of Egypt and the Sinai.[299]

An Egyptian manuscript known as the Ipuwer Papyrus dates between 1550 and 1292 B.C. This manuscript describes a chaotic time in Egypt including drought, starvation, upheaval, and death. Fire and hail are said to have fallen together on Egypt. Such events are unusual circumstances in this part of the world. They may be related to a gigantic volcanic eruption that occurred on the island of Santorini, just off the coast of Egypt.

This is said to have been one of the most powerful eruptions that have ever occurred. The papyrus appears to be an eyewitness account of these tragedies,[300]which by description and antiquity could

126

be referring to the time of the plagues leading to the Exodus. This eruption is considered to have possibly been the cause of some of the plagues such as the "darkness that could be felt" which might have been the result of volcanic ash in the air.[301]

Exodus 13:17 informs us that God did not lead the people of Israel up the direct route into Canaan *"lest they change their minds when they see war and they return to Egypt."* Why the Israelites were led the long way through the Sinai rather than the short direct route and the mention of war were not understood previously, because there were no known people in the Sinai to oppose Israel.

This confusion was resolved by Israeli archaeologist Trude Dothan who discovered an Egyptian outpost built in the fourteenth century on the direct ancient route, and a fortress there from the thirteenth century. It is thought there may have been additional Egyptian outposts as well. This route was protected because it enabled Egypt's military access into Canaan. The probable confrontation with the Egyptian army is why Israel avoided the direct route through Sinai.[302]

Randall Price mentions that traversing through the Sinai is extremely unlikely to leave evidence of the presence of the tent dwelling Israelites because of the constantly shifting sands. He suggests that rock inscriptions would be about the only possible evidence of their having been there.[303]

A confirmation of the trek through the wilderness, however, does exist. It is recorded in Numbers 11 that the people were complaining about missing the food they had in Egypt and all they had now was manna. God then provided quail for them to eat, but in verses 33-35 the text mentions a punishment from the Lord because of their complaining that killed a large number of people.

In the Sinai, on a high mountain, a German explorer, Berthoid Neibuhr, found a huge cemetery in 1761.[304] The tombstones had inscriptions that were different from Egyptian writings though somewhat similar to them. There was no mention of Egyptian gods nor any Egyptian symbols, but there were engravings of quail and mentions of dying due to a plague from Yahweh. A later explorer discovered that the Bedouins called this *"The graveyard of the Jews."*[305]

Earlier in the passage of Numbers 11 it tells of God sending a wind that brought quail which fell outside the Israelites camp. Naturalist Peter Farb mentions that the only migratory quail have weak ability to fly and are often blown off course by wind. He states that they then fall onto the nearest land exhausted. That they fell by the camp in the evening according to the Bible fits as well because these quail usually fly at night. [306] The Biblical account fits with the reality regarding these particular birds.

Exodus 15:1-18 is often referred to as Mariam's song. According to Albright the style, vocabulary and grammar are pre-Mosaic. [307] This is perhaps due to Mariam being Moses older sister. She may have adapted an older known song or older lyrical form to this new situation.

A liberal Introduction to the Old Testament dates the song in the late fifth century B.C. Albright notes that, *"it is absurd to date the Song of Mariam eight centuries too late on the strength of evidence which actually points in the opposite direction."* [308] The song's form is typical of those older than Moses, not later. Liberal bias again distorted the evidence so it appeared to validate their disbelief in the authenticity of the Biblical scriptures.

The Israelite invasion of Canaan seems to be confirmed through the archaeological discovery of at least six cities west of the Jordon River. These cities were destroyed over 3,200 years ago at the time Joshua was said to have led the incursion. Canaan at that time was divided into many fortified city states each with their own king. [309] This division of the Canaanites would have aided conquest by the invading Hebrews under Joshua.

Excavations show massive debris at Debir, Hazor and Lachish from destruction at about the thirteen century B.C. [310] This later date may reflect action of either Israelites or other peoples who are known to have invaded Canaan around 1200 B.C. [311] It might also relate to the time of Judges.

The Egyptian Pharaoh Merneptah conducted a military campaign in 1220 B.C. which resulted in the Hittites giving him Palestine and southern Syria. His monument celebrating this victory was found in Thebes.[312] In part it declares, *"Libya is captured, while Hatti is pacified. Canaan is plundered, Ashkelon is carried off, and Gezer is captured. Yenoam is made into non-existence; Israel is laid waste, its seed is not."*[313]

It is of further significance, as Egyptologist Manfred Bietak states that the names *"Ashkelon, Gezer and Yeno'am are followed by an Egyptian hieroglyph that designates a town, Israel is followed by a hieroglyph that means a people."*[314] This indicates Israel by that time as having been of much more significance than a mere town.

This is the only known mention of Israel on an ancient Egyptian monument. Despite the Pharaoh's excessive boasting, for Israel to be mentioned in the midst of these other known cities is very significant. This proves Israel was a recognized nation in Palestine sometime prior to this Egyptian military campaign. It also indicates they must have had a sizable population to be singled out, otherwise there would be nothing for the Pharaoh to boast about.

What corroborating evidence of the Exodus out of Egypt might we expect to find if the Exodus were a historically true event? What about some kind of evidence of the sudden appearance of the Israelites in Canaan? That would certainly be confirming evidence.

During the 12th and 13th centuries B.C., approximately 300 small settlements appear in the highlands of Judea which significantly increased the population of the region.[315] The attempt is made by critics to explain that these are new Canaanite settlements. However, that does not explain either the sudden significant growth in population nor the distinctive culture of these new settlements. It is important to notice also that these distinctives did not gradually develop over time but are a sharp break from the culture of the surrounding Canaanite settlements!

The Biblical narratives do account for these distinctives, as Dewayne Bryant points out: *"God commanded the Israelites to maintain the difference between themselves and other peoples, including those of Canaan. They were not to take foreign wives, adopt other religious customs, or make treaties with the native populations (Exodus 23:31-33; 34:12-16; Deuteronomy 7:3-6)."* [316]

One of those distinctives is shown in the complete absence of raising or eating pigs in the new settlements. The Canaanites loved pork and raised pigs extensively in their communities. The Israelites were forbidden in the Law of Moses to eat pork (Leviticus 11:1-47; Deuteronomy 14:3-20).

This prohibition accounts for the significant difference in communities established by the Hebrews from that of Canaanite settlements. This difference between the two cultures exists, even when the two settlements were in close proximity.[317] This absence of pigs gives witness that the Hebrews had migrated to Canaan and retained this cultural distinctive in contrast to their Canaanite neighbors.

A second cultural evidence that those new settlements were Israelite and not Canaanite was the sudden arrival of the typical Israelite constructed four room houses in the Judea highlands. This was so typical of Hebrew construction and communities that it has been designated as "the Israelite house." Manfred Bietak found this exact style of construction in the area of Egypt (the Nile Delta) where the Hebrews had lived and at the Hyksos' Egyptian capital at Avaris.[318]

This home construction existed at both locations said to have been inhabited by the Hebrews in Egypt. That construction suddenly appeared in the locations of the new communities formed in the Judean highlands. This is evidence that the Exodus is not fiction but actual history.

The only reasonable explanation for the existence of this unique construction in the area where the Hebrews lived in Egypt and its sudden appearance in Canaan is that the Hebrews escaped from Egypt and migrated into Canaan.

A 1979 discovery of tiny silver scrolls in a tomb near Jerusalem contain the Aaronic benediction (Numbers 6:24-26). This find dates prior to the exile of Judah which disputes critical scholars who claim the Pentateuch was mostly written by priests after the exile.[319]

Danish excavations show that Shiloh was destroyed by the Philistines about or shortly after the middle of the eleventh century B.C. At that time, the Philistines also destroyed many other towns including Debir and Beth-zur.[320]

The background of Deuteronomy 32 has been clarified and confirmed as reliable through recent discoveries of the Sefire treaties and information among the Dead Sea Scrolls according to W.F. Albright.[321] He went on to state that prior assumptions of contradictions in narratives of Samuel are now seen instead *"as essential contributions to the total historical picture."*[322]

For example, Samuel is said to be from the tribe of Ephraim 1Sam. 1:1 and as a Levite in 1 Chron. 6:16-45. The explanation is that as one whose entire life was devoted to the service of God in the Tabernacle, he performed the services of a Levite and was therefore likely considered to be one.[323]

Jericho

In the 1950's the conquest of Jericho by Joshua was declared by archaeologist Kathleen Kenyon to have been impossible. She declared it had been destroyed in the sixteenth century B.C. and that there was no walled city there as depicted in the book of Joshua.[324] The Biblical account was therefore written off by most scholars as religious rhetoric and folklore.[325]

A new comprehensive review of Kenyon's evidence however has led to conclusions that Jericho was a walled city until about 1400 B.C. At that time *"it was destroyed in a conquest strikingly similar to the Biblical account. The 1400 B.C.E. conquest would match the chronology derived from the Bible."*[326] This dating agrees with the earlier dating of the ruins by British archaeologist John Garstang in the 1930's. In harmony with the Biblical account, Garstang concluded the Jericho had been torched about 1400 B.C.[327] (Joshua 6:24)

It is also significant that any military force coming from the east (as from Egypt) would have to deal first with Jericho in order to invade the central hill country of Canaan.[328] This also is in harmony with the Biblical account which records that Jericho was the first conquest in Canaan by Israel (Joshua 2:1; 3:16).

Part of the discrepancy between Kenyon's reports and those of Garstang were due to much of her excavations being in a different sector of Jericho. She had assumed from her work that Garstang and the Bible were wrong. Kenyon also basically ignored the local pottery at the site. Instead, she emphasized the absence of pottery imported from Cyprus that had been previously found at Megiddo. *"In other words, Kenyon's analysis was based upon what was not found at Jericho rather than what was found."*[329]

The more recent research regarding Jericho also reveals that pottery discovered by Garstang dates to 1550-1400 B.C., precisely the period Kenyon repeatedly declared that there was no population at Jericho. It is difficult to explain why Kenyon ignored the locally made pottery. Her conclusions were also based upon a very limited excavation site in the poorer section of the town.[330]

The dating of Jericho's destruction around 1400 B.C. was further substantiated by a Carbon-14 dating of charcoal from the burning of the city during the final Bronze Age. This indicated a date of 1410 B.C. with an error range of plus or minus 40 years. This is not even close to the 1550 B.C. dating Kenyon gave for the destruction of the city.

The evidence indicates the city was destroyed in a major calamity. The walls of Jericho did collapse as Joshua records. The amount of bricks suggests a wall six and a half feet wide and twelve feet high.[331] Also the ancient ruins give evidence the city was torched after the walls had collapsed, which also agrees with the sequence in Joshua.

Both Kenyon and Garstang found extensive stored grain in their excavations. *"The ample food supply at Jericho indicates that it succumbed quickly not after a long siege; and this occurred after harvest not before."* [332] (See Joshua 3:15). Thus, many specific details of the more recent reevaluation of the evidence would seem to substantiate the Biblical account of the destruction of Jericho. [333]

The United Kingdom

The Bible informs us that Israel's first king, Saul was from Gibeah. Saul kept his headquarters there after becoming king. Albright himself excavated King Saul's fortress at Gibeah, which he felt had probably been originally a Philistine fort. [334]

The records of Saul's death by the Philistines were thought by skeptics, to be contradictory. 1 Samuel 31:10 indicated that Saul's armor was placed in the temple of Ashtaroth, who was a Canaanite goddess, and that his body was fastened to the wall at Bethshan. 1 Chronicles 10:10 says that Saul's head was hung in the temple of Dagon who was a god of the Philistines. The assumption was that there would not have been temples of opposing peoples in the same nation at the same time and in proximity, so at least one of these statements had to be an error.

Then the city was excavated by Alan Rowe in the 1930's. A Canaanite temple and a Philistine one were found adjoined at the same level of excavation. [335] A common ancient pagan practice was to accept gods of a defeated peoples into your own pantheon so as not to risk the wrath of the local deity. This is apparently what had happened. The Biblical writers had again been vindicated, and the critics refuted.

Critics known as minimalists have claimed that King David and his reign were mythical creations. They have assumed that the Biblical stories of David and Solomon were legends developed from heroic traditions and that there never was a unified monarchy.[336] Archaeologist Kathleen Kenyon wrote in 1987 that it was surprising that, *"No extra-Biblical inscription, either from Palestine or from a neighboring country has yet been found to contain a reference to them."*[337]

Structures related to the time of David have been excavated in Jerusalem showing the Hebrew presence there at that time. Ten years after Kenyon wrote a reference was found referring to "the House of David."[338] This is on a 3,000-year-old black basalt stele found at the ancient site of Dan in northern Israel. It is designated the Tel Dan Stele. This stele written in Aramaic refers to eight kings referenced in the Bible.[339]

Included in the Aramaic inscription is a statement that reads, *"I killed Jehoram son of Ahab king of Israel and I killed Ahaziahu son of Jehoram king of the House of David."*[340] "House of ..." is a dynastic term referring the founder of that line of rulers. [341] This is strong evidence of the existence of the historical king David.

The stele, inscribed by one of Israel's enemies, refers to historical events recorded in the Bible (2 Kings 8:7-15; 9:6-10). It is commemorating the victory of King Ben Hadad of Damascus over Jehoram, king of Israel and a "king of the House of David." This would be about 150 years after David's time and the king was identified as Judah's king, Ahaziah.[342] This confirms some Biblical events as well as kings' names given in the Old Testament.

Some critics try to explain away the reference to David or translate the inscription differently to avoid the evidence. This is because their assumptions often take precedence over historical evidence. These

135

alternate interpretations can find no justification in archaeology or history.[343]

Another difficulty facing those who wish to dismiss David as a mere myth or legend is the actual presentation of David in the Bible. Mythic persons, other than the false gods, are usually presented as wholly good and admirable. In contrast alongside his passion for God, David is shown to be guilty of pride, fear, laziness, infidelity, murder, and a failure as a father. This portrayal is realistic and true to life rather than fitting the picture we are usually given of legendary persons.

There are also some scholars that will admit the existence of David and Solomon, but discount the importance of the Biblical accounts of their exploits. These critics declare that Israel was a very small and unimportant entity. For example, Israeli archaeologist Israel Finkelstein argues that, *"David and Solomon did not rule over a big territory. It was a small chiefdom, if you wish, with just a few settlements, very poor, the population was limited, there was no manpower for a big conquest ..."*[344]

In contrast to this perspective, are the Amarna Letters of the fourteen century B.C. between Egyptian officials and Canaanite city-states. The letters indicate that Jerusalem is a significant city at that time.[345] In addition other cities like Megiddo, Hazor, and Gezer have massive city gates [346] which would indicate significant size and importance.

A French scholar believes he has found a second reference to the "House of David" in a formerly illegible line on the Moabite Sone.[347] This monument was set up by King Mesha of Moab about the middle or late ninth century B.C. to celebrate his victory over Israel. This stele contains confirmation of other information given in 1 Kings and 2 Kings.

136

Scholars have accepted the existence of Omri king of Israel because he is mentioned on the Moabite stone discovered in the nineteenth century. They reject David's mention because their minds were made up prior to the more recent discoveries. Interestingly, Assyrian texts use the phrases "the land of Omri" and "House of Omri" in regard to the Northern Kingdom even a hundred years after his death. This indicates the use of such terms to refer to a dynasty's founder and supports that meaning in the reference to the "House of David." In the more recent discovery. [348]

Archaeologist Bryant Wood stated, *"Many times the newer discoveries of archaeology have overturned older critical views of the Bible. Many scholars have said there never was a David or Solomon, and now we have a stele that actually mentions David."* [349]

It has been claimed by critics that the Jewish temple, said to have been built by Solomon in Jerusalem, never existed. Later building of the second and third temples on the same location has eclipsed most, if not all of the evidence of the earlier construction. This is partly due to reusing the surviving building material. Competing religious claims have also hindered excavating the area. Especially as the Islamic Dome of the Rock now covers most of the original temple site, any kind of recent excavation is impossible.

The only known item discovered from the first temple is an eighth century B.C. ivory pomegranate from the tip of a scepter. An inscription on the pomegranate links it to use in the temple. The second temple was not built for another two centuries after the first was destroyed.

However, Solomon was involved in extensive construction projects in addition to the original Israelite temple. His fortifications of Gezer, Megiddo and Hazor have been excavated as has his copper refineries at Ezion-geber at the north end of the Gulf of Aqabah. [350] According to 1 Kings 10:26-29, Solomon acquired a great number of horses and chariots which were mostly purchased from Egypt. These were stationed in other major cities as well as Jerusalem. Albright informs us Solomon's well-built stalls for horses found at Megiddo are said to number approximately 450.[351]

The Kingdom Divided

Soon after Solomon's death in 922 B.C., the kingdom divided into two weaker nations. Ten tribes revolted under Jeroboam against Solomon's son, Rehoboam. The ten tribes became known as, the Northern Kingdom or Israel. The Southern kingdom of Judah was comprised of Judah and Benjamin.

Fearful that his people might rejoin Judah because the temple and all the festivals were celebrated in Jerusalem, Jeroboam created two rival centers of worship. These two centers were at the extremities of the Northern Kingdom, Dan in the north and Bethel in the south. A seal of Shema *"Servant of Jeroboam"* was found at Megiddo.

Though it is uncertain which Jeroboam is meant, it is most likely that this is a seal belonging to an official in the government of Jeroboam I who ruled as the first of the Northern Kingdom's kings (926-904 B.C.). [352] That early dating is based upon the level at which the seal was found, its art style and paleography.[353]

Jeroboam's symbols for worship were two golden calves, reminiscent of the idolatry Aaron instigated at Sinai while Moses was up on the Mount. This may have been an attempt to give some semblance of a historical connection to Israel's past for the idolatry he was establishing. His choice of Bethel also had significant historical connections for the people. This initiation of idolatry by their king, Jeroboam appears to have permanently led the vast majority of Israel astray. The Northern Kingdom's kings were all corrupt and ungodly.

Unfortunately, the apostasy in the Northern Kingdom, and the repeated vacillation between Yahweh and idolatry in Judah were the fruition of paganizing influences allowed and promoted during Solomon's reign through his pagan foreign wives and his own defection from Yahweh.

Extensive excavations at the base of Mount Hermon have led to the discovery of the sanctuary in Dan built by Jeroboam.[354] Cultic ritual items were found there including incense stands and shovels, a horned alter, and a figurine of Astarte. An inscription also found at the site states "to the god who is in Dan."[355] In the Northern Kingdom's ancient capital of Samaria, a small bull idol was also found at what had probably served as a 'high place.'[356]

King Ahab of Israel married Princess Jezebel, the daughter of Ittobaal (Ethbaal), the king of Tyre, thus cementing an alliance with the Phoenicians. Phoenician religion came to dominate the Northern Kingdom from that relationship. Excavations at Samaria reveal that great wealth had resulted from the trade between the two countries.[357] The frequency of names containing Baal indicates the influence of Baal worship in the Northern Kingdom.[358]

An event not mentioned in the Bible lists Ahab in an alliance resisting the westward advance of Assyria.[359] Shalmaneser's stele recounting the event lists "Ahab the Israelite" and his 2,000 chariots and 10,000-foot soldiers.[360]

1 Kings 16 attributes more evil to Ahab than any of the preceding kings of Israel. The great drought and famine of Ahab's time is also recorded in Tyre's

annals.[361]   Ahab was killed in battle against Bed-Hadad of Aram at Ramoth-gilead on the northeastern frontier of Israel (2 Chronicles 18:33-34). Albright mentions Nelson Glueck's discovery of that location.[362]

Jeroboam established the capital of the Northern Kingdom in Tirzah. This had been a Canaanite city until conquered by Joshua (Joshua 12:24). It remained the capital until Omri built Samaria and moved the capital there (1 Kings 16:23-24). Archaeology identifies Tirzah as modern tell el-fara. It was a large city that goes back to before 3000 B.C. Sometime before 600 B.C. it was abandoned.[363]

How the Moabites became subjected to the Northern Kingdom of Israel is not mentioned in the Bible. A victory stele, known as the Moabite Stone indicates they were conquered by Omri. Mesha, the king of Moab, is recounting Moab's successful revolt from Israel after the death of Ahab (2 Kings 3). The inscribed stone was discovered in Dhiban, a Moabite city east of the Dead Sea in 1868.[364]

Amos 6:1-7 mentions the luxury and the debauchery of Samaria's officials including having beds of ivory. The ostraca excavated there from about the middle of the eighth century B.C. or earlier suggest that the common people were being required to pay for this luxury. Along with the ostraca several hundred pieces of ivory were also excavated. Some of the ivory had obviously been used as inlays in furniture.[365]

Also, a stele of Ben-hadad, who was the enemy of both Israel and the Phoenicians was found dated about 850 B.C. The stele includes a dedication to Baal-Melcarth one of the Phoenicians major gods.[366] The stele indicates the same line of succession in Syria as given in 1 Kings 15:16-18. The stele verifies not only the historicity of the people and events indicated in the Biblical passage, but also indicates the pagan influence of Phoenicia extended beyond the boundary of Israel to at least Syria. There are at least two and possibly three persons in the Old Testament named Ben-hadad.[367]

The prophet Elisha told Hazael that he would be king over Aram (Syria) and would be cruel as he conquered cities in Israel (2 Kings 8:7-15). Hazael murdered Ben-hadad and took over as king at about 841 B.C. Assyrian records refer to Hazael seizing the throne and raising an army against Assyria. The record states that Assyria defeated Hazael.[368] Hazael's name also occurs in several other documents including one in 841 B.C. where Shalmaneser reported attacking Hazael.[369]

King Jehu of Israel became a vassal of Shalmaneser at approximately 841 B.C. On another stele, Jehu is portrayed on his knees before Shalmaneser. The stele also mentions the specific tribute received from Jehu.[370]

Hazael's son Ben-hadad II or III (?) succeeded him around 801 B.C. (2 Kings 13:24). The Aramaic Zakir inscription refers to the succession and records the deliverance of Zakir, king of Hamath, from a coalition united against him by Ben-hadad, son of Hazael.[371] The various sequence of kings faced by Joash, king of Israel (801-786 B.C.) is also confirmed by the Zakir inscription.[372] A stele found in 1967 at Tell al Rimah near Mosel, Iraq, shows king Adad-nirari III with text including references to Samaria and King Joash.[373]

Rezin became king of Syria approximately 750 B.C. He allied with Syria's former enemy, Israel, against Ahaz, king of Judah (2 Kings 15:37). Fearful and contrary to the advice of Isaiah, Ahaz used the temple treasure to hire Assyria's Tiglath-pileser to attack Syria and Israel (Isa. 7:1-4). Judah was spared, but the people of

Damascus and part of the Northern Kingdom were exiled by Tiglath-pileser and Rezin was killed (2 Kings 15:29; 16:9).

An Assyrian text mentions receiving tribute from Rezin.[374] The Assyrian annals are mutilated at this point but mention Rezin fleeing Damascus as the Assyrians capture the city and his main advisors being impaled.[375]

Hoshea was the Northern Kingdom's final king (732-722 B.C.). His royal signet seal has been discovered through archaeology. It reveals the persistent apostasy that finally brought about the destruction of the kingdom. The seal mentions Hoshea by name and *"depicts an Egyptian figure standing above a solar disc (a symbol of the god Ra)."* [376]

The Apocryphal book of Tobit confirms information in the Bible about the dispersion of much of the people of the Northern Kingdom by Assyria. Assyrian inscriptions mention settlement of exiles from Israel in Media.[377]

Hezekiah became king of Judah during the rule of Hoshea and saw the conquest of the Northern Kingdom by Assyria. He was a godly king. His renewal efforts included missionary efforts among the remnants of Israelites still living in the Northern Kingdom (2 Chronicles 30). This must have been opposed by the Assyrian governors because Assyrian records indicate there was difficulty keeping the Israelite population under control.[378]

The Phoenician king of Ashdod, then their most important city, sought aid from Judah's king, Hezekiah, and from Egypt in a rebellion against Assyria. In 711 B.C. Ashdod was conquered and made an Assyrian province and Egyptian aid was a complete failure. Inscriptions of Sargon II verify this conquest in 712 or 711 B.C.[379] This elicited a response from Isaiah about the vein hope in Egypt (Isaiah 20) as well as taunts from the Assyrian historian of the time. [380] Hezekiah had apparently avoided this disastrous alliance.

However, about ten years later Hezekiah did get involved in another rebellion instigated by Merodach-baladan of Babylon and by Egypt. He fortified Jerusalem and intervened in Phoenicia. The Assyrians reinvaded in 701 B.C. crushing the revolt and defeating a large Egyptian and Ethiopian Army. This is also when Judah's fortress of Lachish was taken and many other cities defeated, leading to Hezekiah's capitulation to Assyrian king Sennacherib. These victories, as well as the heavy tribute levied upon Hezekiah, are listed in Assyrian records.[381]

Josiah, the great grandson of Hezekiak, was the last godly king of Judah. He became king at eight and at age twenty he began to purge Judah of the rampant idolatry of the previous fifty years (2 Chronicles 34). Evidence of the extent of his destruction of idol worship has been found at Ein Hatzeva, the Biblical site of Tamar (Ezekiel 47:19). This is in the desert about 32 miles south of the Dead Sea.

This site had apparently served as a roadside cultic high place. An Edomite shrine there was discovered to have been deliberately demolished at near the end of the first temple era, which would have been during Josiah's reign.[382]

Over seventy pottery and cultic stone objects were lying under the rocks that had been used to demolish them. The destroyed cultic items included statues, alters, chalices, libation vessels, incense burners, etc. The thoroughness of Josiah's renewal is indicated by this destruction so far south in Judah.[383]

Josiah's reforms are said to have extended to the defunct Northern Kingdom's center of idolatrous worship at Bethel as well as the other towns of Samaria (2 Kings 23:15-20). This action shows not only his fervor for Yahweh, but also concern and perhaps hope of reuniting the remnants of Israel and Judah[384]

Unfortunately, this renewal, despite its thoroughness during Josiah's reign, did not last. Many idols and cultic items have been found, especially in Jerusalem itself. These items reveal the return to idolatry after his death that preceded Judah's destruction and exile.

In 609 B.C. Josiah unwisely sought to prevent pharaoh Necho from joining Assyria in its battle for survival against Babylon (2 Kings 23:29-30). Judean forces were crushed by Necho and Josiah was killed. These events are confirmed in the Babylonian Chronicles.[385]

Early Egyptian persons are only identified in the Bible by their title. The earliest pharaoh mentioned by name in the Bible is Shoshenq, given in the Bible as Shishak. He attacked and defeated Judah shortly after the death of Solomon about 918 B.C. (1 Kings 14:25-26). The division of the Hebrews into two weaker nations appears to have strengthened Shishak's aspirations for conquest.

Shishak claimed to have successfully defeated over 150 cities in Palestine. He then set up a monument at the south entrance of the temple of his god in Karnak, Egypt, to commemorate his victories.

This monument lists cities of Judah, Israel, and Edom.[386] Though Shishak may have exaggerated his successes, excavations have shown the destruction at that time of a number of the cities he claims to have destroyed.[387] A fragment of a Shishak victory stele has been discovered at Megiddo, one of the towns listed at Karnak as having been conquered by him.[388] The fragment also clearly lists the name Shoshenq.

144

Assyria Becomes Dominant

2 Kings 19:8-9 mentions Tirhakah, king of Cush (Ethiopia and Egypt), came out to battle Sennacherib, king of Assyria, who had been conquering the cities of Judah. Hezekiah was the king of Judah at this time. The Bible has again been vindicated as accurately presenting historical names and events. Five Steles of Tirhakah have been excavated as well as Assyrian records of success in fighting against him by both Sennacherib and Esarhaddon.[389]

Pharaoh Necho, whose army killed king Josiah of Judah (2 Chronicles 35:20-24), is mentioned by the historian Herodotus. Necho is also referred to by the first century A.D. Jewish historian Josephus and on fragments of a stele found at Sidon.[390]

Assyria became a danger about the beginning of the ninth century B.C., defeating and replacing Egypt as the dominant power in the Middle East. In 853 B.C. Assyria first came into direct conflict with Israel. King Ahab faced Shallmaeser III. From 747 to 626 B.C. every Assyrian king is correctly mentioned in the Bible. [391]

Also, it is known that the Assyrian monarch known as Pul and Tiglath-pileser III in the Old Testament is the same king. We know these are the same person because he is called by one name in the Babylonian Chronicles and by the other in the Babylonian list of kings.[392] His palace was discovered in the mid-1800's. His successors followed the policy he initiated of removing large proportions of conquered populations.

This population removal included the Syrians and the Northern Kingdom of Israel. Tiglath-pileser is mentioned outside of the Bible in regard to Judah's king Azariah and others including Menahem, Ahaz, Pekah and Hoshea.[393]

The son of Tiglath-pileser, Shalmaneser V, succeeded

his father as king and as recipient of tribute from Hoshea, king of Israel. Shalmaneser imprisoned Hoshea for attempting to revolt and exiled more of Israel's population in 722 B.C. The Babylonian Chronicles and several monuments give us further information of his activities and mention his palace.[394]

Archaeology has proven that Sargon II of Assyria was not an imaginary creation of Isaiah, as skeptics previously claimed. Critics had confidently declared there was no such king. Sargon II is only mentioned once in scripture (Isa. 20:1). Even Isaiah's use of the title "Commander-in-chief" was found to be accurate.[395] A fragment of Sargon's stele celebrating his conquest of Ashdod was found at that site, confirming Isaiah's statement regarding that exact campaign.[396]

Sargon succeeded Shalmaneser as king of Assyria. The palace that he erected for himself at Khorsabad has been discovered. Sargon claimed credit for the victory over Israel, but archaeology has confirmed the Bible in attributing the victory to Shalmaneser. Sargon apparently completed the exile project after Shalmaneser's death.[397]

Sennacherib became king of Assyria in 705 B.C. and invaded Judah four years later. He took over some of Judah's fortified cities and began a siege of Lachish. Sennacherib's Annals describe his campaign against Judah and Hezekiah, but do not mention the second phase in which his army was destroyed. [398] Sennacharib's Annals mention that he has Jerusalem surrounded and in a hopeless situation and that Judah's king Hezekiah is shut in like a bird in a cage. He gave no explanation for lifting the siege and his return to Nineveh (Isa. 36-37).[399]

Herodotus relates the destruction of the Assyrian army, but does not attribute the disaster to the intervention of God. Instead, he declares hordes of mice invaded the Assyrian camp and devoured their bows, quivers, and shield's handles. Herodotus said as a result of this the Assyrian army fled and many were killed.[400] At some point after this disaster the Babylonian Chronicle states that in 681 B.C. during a rebellion, Sennacherib was killed by his son. This is in substantial agreement with the Bible that gives two of his sons as the murders (2 Kings 18-19).[401]

Following Sennacherib's assassination by his sons, a third son, Esarhaddon becomes the king of Assyria (2 Kings 19:37). The Babylonian Chronicles account is very similar to that in the Bible. Esarhaddon forced vassal treaties upon Iran requiring them at his death to support the accession of his sons to the thrones of Assyria and Babylon. *"Scholars have been quick to call attention to the parallels in the form of these vassal treaties to Old Testament covenants."* [402] Even the Old Testament covenants are known to be culturally appropriate for their era.

The last significant Assyrian king is Asherbanipal who is mentioned by name only once in the Old Testament which gives his name as Osnappar (Ezra 4:9-10). There is however an indirect reference to his destruction of Thebes, Egypt, in Nahum 3:8ff. [403] Manasseh, the king of Judah, is listed in an ancient extra-Biblical reference as among those forced to accompany and aid in this successful attack on Egypt. [404] Ashherbanipal is also the unnamed king who imports foreign peoples into Samaria (2 Kings 17:24).[405]

At the height of Assyria's might, Nahum predicted in great detail in 663 B.C. that Nineveh would be destroyed and not heard of again. Zephaniah in 625 B.C. added that Nineveh would become a desolate habitation of only beasts and birds.

It happened as predicted in 612 B.C. Modern excavations have confirmed that everything at Sennacherib's palace had been burned, looted, or destroyed. Animals made their homes in the mound of the once powerful city. [406] Nineveh's sudden destruction and disappearance from history is specifically recounted in the Babylonian Chronicles. [407]

Lachish was a very significant fortified city in Judah. The Lachish Mural consists of a series of relief sculptures depicting the battle between the people of Lachish and the Assyrian army during the conquest of that city in 701 B.C. The sculptures were discovered in a palace room of king Sennacherib's at Nineveh. This exact event is mentioned in 2 Kings 7:5-6 and 2 Chronicles 32:1, 9. (See also Isaiah 36:1-2). [408] In this particular case archaeology has made it possible to actually see portrayed an important historical event referenced in the Bible. The panels of this historical event are now in the British Museum.

Another discovery made in Nineveh was an actual written version of the Assyrian invasion of Judah in 701 B.C. known as the Taylor Prism. [409] In the account, Sennacherib does not claim to have captured Jerusalem, but neither does he mention the calamity the Assyrian Army experienced (2 Kings 18:13 - 19:37). He does not comment on why the siege of Jerusalem was discontinued.

Babylonian Supremacy

2 Kings 20:12 states that about 702 B.C. Merodach-baladan, the king of Babylon, sent Hezekiah letters and a present on hearing of Hezekiah's recovery from a severe illness. This king is well documented in history beginning in the annals of Tiglath-pileser, the Nimrud letters and many other places including the Babylonian Chronicles. [410] The Babylonians were

asserting themselves against Assyria and were encouraging Assyria's vassal states to rebel. This revolt is asserted by Josephus to be the true motive of Merodach-Baladan's contact with Hezekiah.[411]

The Babylonian Chronicles are among some 90,000 clay tablets received by the British Museum between 1872 and 1889. Most of these overwhelming amounts of cuneiform texts have not been translated. Those which have been translated have proved to be precise, accurate Babylonian records of historical events relating to significant events during the reigns of various Babylonian kings.[412]

The nine clay tablets Donald Wiseman published in 1956 from among these Chronicles contain details involving the conquest of Judah by Babylon. Those details include the Babylonian king (Nebuchadnezzar) replacing Judah's king (Jehoiachin) with his own choice of king (Zedekiah) and taking huge tribute back to Babylon (2 Kings 24:1-13).[413] According to the Babylonian record this conquest of Judah took place in 597 B.C.

The Lachish Letters are ostraca recovered near the gate of the city of Lachish which record some of the tragedy of the siege and conquest of that city in 586 B.C. only 25 miles from Jerusalem.[414] Lachish's military commander is depicted on one ostracon as crying out for help as the Babylonian army approached.[415] No help came, and after Lachish, the Babylonians marched right on into Jerusalem and put it to the torch.

Prior to 587 B.C. king Jehoiachin along with his family, Judah's military, its leading men, and best craftsmen were taken to Babylon by Nebuchadnezzar (2 Kings 24:16). Zedekiah was made king over Judah. Later he rebelled and Jerusalem was again put under siege and again taken by Nebuchadnezzar. More captives were taken to Babylon including Zedekiah.

Another defeat of Egypt and Pharaoh Necho is presented in Jeremiah 46 as coming at the hands of Babylon. Nebuchadnezzar defeated Necho's large army in the famous battle of Carchemish in 605 B.C. This is reported in both the Babylonian Chronicles and by Josephus. Necho's name also appears on a stele at Sidon.[416]

The last connection of the Old Testament with a named ruler of Egypt is with Pharaoh Hophra (ruled 588-569 B.C.). Jeremiah declared Hophra to be a false hope for Judah against Babylon and that the Lord would give Hophra over to Babylon (Jeremiah 44:30). Hophra is mentioned by the ancient historians: Herodotus in his <u>Histories</u> and Diodorus' <u>Library of History</u>. [417] Under Nebuchadnezzar, Hophra was defeated as Jeremiah had predicted. Babylon took over all territory previously under Egyptian control east of the river of Egypt.[418]

Nebuchadnezzar's boast of rebuilding Babylon was unknown outside of the Bible (Daniel 4:30) until verified by modern excavations.[419]

King Nebuchadnezzar is mentioned more than ninety times and receives more space in the Bible than any other non-Jewish monarch. He deported people from Judah in 597 and 586 B.C. He appears frequently as the enemy of Israel in the apocryphal and rabbinic literature as well.[420] The names of king Nabopolassar and his son Nebuchadnezzar were found stamped into a Babylonian brick. [421] The extensive building projects of Nebuchadnezzar, including the famous hanging gardens, are well documented from excavations.[422]

The ancient Phoenician city of Tyre was prophesied against by Ezekiel about 592 B.C. (Ezekial 26-28). The prophecy is detailed and includes the statement from

God saying *"I will bring up many nations against you ..."* Philostratos' <u>History of Phoenicia</u> is the source Josephus claims for his statement that Nebuchadnezzar besieged the mainland city for 13 years, finally destroying it as was predicted of him.[423]

Over 250 years later, Alexander the Great besieged the island city in 332 B.C. and captured it by building a causeway 200 feet wide out to the island with the remains of the mainland city. As predicted by Ezekiel, the stones, timber, and debris were thrown into the water[424] (Ezekiel 26:3-14).

Despite a slight recovery, Tyre never regained its prior greatness. It was attacked and nearly destroyed again by Muslims in 1291 A.D. Modern Tyre is a fishing town south of the original site. Fisherman spread their nets to dry at the remains of the ancient site of Tyre as Ezekiel declared.[425]

In 562 B.C. Evil-Merodach (Awel-Marduk), the son of Nebuchadnezzar, succeeded his father as king of Babylon (2 Kings 25:27). This is confirmed by a basalt stele as well as by Josephus.[426] He was assassinated after two years and replaced by Nergalsharezer, apparently the son-in-law of Nebuchadnezzar. He is listed among the princes of Babylon's king in Jeremiah 39:3. [427] A prominent landowner prior to becoming king, Nergalsharezer's name shows up in building inscriptions and contract tablets as well as in the list of Babylonian kings.[428]

The book of Daniel purports to describe events during the prominence of Babylon until its conquest in 539 B.C. by the Medes and Persians. The major view of critics however is that Daniel is a disguised account of the Maccabean era around the middle of the second century B. C.[429] This is a rather esoteric attempt to discount the authenticity and significance of this book. It is difficult to account for the Babylonian as well as Persian influence in Daniel if it was not written until about 164 B.C. If it were written that late it would reflect Greek influence rather than the Babylonian and Persian.

The accuracy of Daniel's prophetic element was a huge factor in critics dating the book so late. It was assumed by them that accurate prophecy could not be genuine, so the book had to be written after the events described. [430] Aramaic portions of the book were also asserted to require a very late date. However, the Elephantine Papyri, discovered at a Jewish settlement in Egypt, were written in Aramaic. These are known to be from the fifth century B.C., invalidating the necessity of a late date for Daniel.[431]

Critics claimed that Daniel was in error in its presenting Belshazzar as the final king of Babylon and in stating that he was killed in the Medio-Persian conquest of Babylonian empire (Daniel 5). Secular records had indicated that Nabonidus was the final king. Then the Nabonidus Chronicle was excavated as well as other clay tablets [432] indicating that King Nabonidus (556-539 B.C.) had made his son, the Crown Prince Belshazzar, co-regent, left him in charge and spent most of the last ten years of his reign in Arabia. [433] How did Daniel know about this?

This discovery made sense of the statement in Daniel 4:7 which records Belshazzer offering to make anyone who could translate the mysterious handwriting on the wall to become *"the third highest ruler in the kingdom."* We now know Belshazzer was the second highest ruler and that he was killed during the defeat of Babylon. King Nabonidus, the highest ruler, returned to Babylon in 539 B.C. and was captured by Cyrus' general Gobryas during the takeover of Babylon.[434] Daniel has been completely vindicated.

The complete destruction of Jerusalem by the

Babylonians was accomplished in July-August 587 B.C. This resulted in the exiling of the remaining notables and craftsmen to Babylon. The assassination of the Babylonian appointed governor, Gedaliah, many of his supporters, as well as the Babylonians stationed in Mizpah, resulted in a third deportation to Babylon.

Albright states that Jeremiah 52:28-30 is an extract from an official Babylonian document listing the total number of those deported (4,600 total).[435] More had been killed and a large number fled to Egypt. However, the total deported according to 2 Kings was 10,000 which is over twice as many.

Albright mentions that the discrepancy in the numbers between 2 Kings and Jeremiah assumes that the number in Jeremiah might be a rough estimate (so could the number in 2 Kings). He also thinks the number in 2 Kings was prior to knowing how many of the starving and weakened Israelites died on the long trek from Jerusalem to Babylon.[436] Another unknown factor is whether women and children were included in the 2 Kings' account and only adult men in the Babylonian account Jeremiah quotes.

Jehoiachin and his family are among those mentioned in the royal archives of Nebuchadnezzar as receiving rations from his royal court. Official Babylonian documents also still referred to Jehoiachin as "king of Judah."[437]

Document Seals

According to archaeological discoveries, most if not all of Judah's fortified cities were razed to the ground. Jerusalem and the first temple were destroyed in the fire set by the Babylonians. However, preserved through that fire were clay seals from the various documents which had perished in the fire. These were discovered in 1982. These seals, technically called "bulla," were inscribed with the names of those who had originated the documents that had been destroyed by fire.

Price wrote, "*Seldom does archaeology reveal artifacts bearing the names of people mentioned in the Bible, but among these bullae was found the bulla of 'Gemaryahu [Gemariah] the son of Shaphan.'*" [438] This was a scribe during the reign of King Jehoiakim who is mentioned by Jeremiah. This scribe advised the king against burning Jeremiah's prophecies which the king hated because they predicted God's judgement against Judah (Jeremiah 36:10-12, 25-26).

Many other bulla have been found related to the final years before the Babylonian destruction of Jerusalem. There is one inscribed with the name of Ishmael, the assassin of the Babylonian appointed governor of Judah, Gedaliah. [439] Another has the name "Berekhyahu [Baruch] son of Neriyahu [Neriah] the scribe." [440] Baruch was the personal scribe and companion of Jeremiah (Jeremiah 36:4, 32).

A more recent bulla discovery was made in the area known as the City of David in Jerusalem. This bulla is inscribed "*Nathan-Melech, Servant of the King.*" Servant of the king was used to refer to very loyal officials. This person is mentioned in 2 Kings 23:11 and was one of king Josiah's court officials who participated in Josiah's restoration of Yahweh worship in Judah. It dates between the mid-7th century to the early 6th century B.C. [441]

In 2005 Israeli archaeologist Eilat Mazar was excavating an area north of the City of David in Jerusalem. One of her team spotted a bulla which after careful examination revealed the statement "*Belonging to Yehuchal ben (son of) Shelemiyahu ben Shovi.*" [442] These names were unfamiliar to her but, except for the grandfather's name, were found to occur in Jeremiah 37 and 38. Yehuchal was one of the king's ministers. This bulla was in the layer just prior to the destruction of the first temple by the Babylonians.[443]

Israeli archaeologist Gabriel Barkay's team excavated several rare, previously undiscovered tombs in Jerusalem. In one of them, cave 25, was found two rolled up silver foil plaques covered with characters in ancient Hebrew. They *"discovered that on both amulets we have a text which is almost similar to the book of Numbers 6:24-26, known as the priestly benediction which is used in Jewish prayers and in Christian liturgy ... These are the earliest Biblical verses that we own, and they predate the famous Dead Sea Scrolls by several centuries ..."*[444]

Archaeologist and Egyptologist K.A. Kitchen summarizes the evidence regarding the Biblical record of the final years of the kingdom of Judah: *"The combined data of texts, seals and archaeological contexts suffice to indicate the realities behind the Hebrew accounts of the last decade of the kingdom of Judah."* [445] In this area as well, the Old Testament writings are validated as reliable.

Daniel And The Rise Of Persia

Attacks and criticisms of the book of Daniel have been especially severe. Nebuchadnezzar's madness was dismissed as confusion with a tradition about Nabonidus which is apparently referred to in a non-Biblical Dead Sea Scroll.[446] However, ancient sources refer to a severe illness shortly before Nebuchadnezzar's death.[447]

Another issue critics have made is over Daniel's reference to Darius the Mede (5:31). Darius is thought by many scholars to be unhistorical. This is as yet

155

unresolved, but the other cases where Daniel has been vindicated makes it reasonable to assume that we are merely lacking sufficient information in this case.[448] Also the discovery of a text of Nabonidus from 546 B.C. refers to the "King of the Medes." This has caused some scholars to consider whether Darius is another name for Cyrus.[449]

A more recent and probably reliable explanation is that Darius ruled the Medes and Cyrus the Persians as allies until Darius died two years after the overthrow of Babylon and the two thrones were united in Cyrus. [450] The *"Greek historian Xenophon describes a Median king, whom he calls Cyaxares II, who corresponds very closely to Daniel's Darius the Mede."[451]*

That Cyaxares II was the same person as Darius was the standard Jewish and Christian position until the 1870's. That view was discarded because cuneiform inscriptions were found that seemed to support Herodotus' account of Cyrus accession which excluded Cyaxares II.[452]

However, it has been found the Xenophon has been more accurate in his information about Belshazzar, Cyrus and the confederation between the Medes and Persians than Herodotus. The Medes and Persians were not only allies, but Cyrus married the daughter of Cyaxares II.[453]

Archaeological discoveries have confirmed the edict of Cyrus (538 B.C.) given in Ezra 1:1-4 to be consistent with other edicts which he ordered during his reign.[454] His edict allowed and promoted the rebuilding of the temple in Jerusalem and gave permission for Jews to return to the land of Israel. The Cyrus Cylinder doesn't specifically mention the Jews, but shows that allowing return and restoration was his general policy.[455]

Ezra also states that Cyrus returned all *"the articles belonging to the temple of the Lord, which Nebuchadnezzar had carried away from Jerusalem and had placed in the temple of his god."* (Ezra 1:7). The restoration of these temple objects had been prophesied by both Isaiah (52:1-12) one hundred fifty years earlier, and again more recently by Jeremiah (27:16 - 28:6).

Other edicts of Cyrus have been found recorded on a stone cylinder that provides close parallels to that recorded by Ezra.[456] On the cylinder is recorded that Cyrus ordered all stolen sacred temple objects be restored, that people be allowed to return to their prior homelands and their sacred sanctuaries restored.[457] This is an example showing that archaeology sometimes reveals the fulfillment of Biblical prophecy!

Ezra mentions the kings Darius, Xerxes, and Artaxerxes (Ezra 4:5-11) in relation to the rebuilding of the temple and efforts to hinder that reconstruction by the peoples transplanted in Israel by Esarhaddon.

Sculpted figures and cuneiform inscriptions 300 feet above an ancient caravan trail in Iran were wondered at for centuries. This mountain is known as the Rock of Behistan. The sculpted figures include Darius the Great, ruler of the Persian Empire (522-486 B.C.), and a dozen other men. The inscriptions mention Darius' sons, Xerxes and Darius Hystaspes, who aided the Jews return to Judah and the rebuilding of the temple.[458]

This was the first primary evidence of this Darius outside of the Old Testament. It also proved the existence of Xerxes, the Ahasuerus of the Bible, who married Esther, and the existence of Artaxerxes.[459]

Xerxes is a Greek rendition of the king named Ahasuerus in the book of Esther. He is called Xerxes in Ezra 4:6. He was a son of Darius, chosen over his brothers by Darius to rule next. He is proclaimed on a doorjamb of the palace in Persepolis.[460] He is shown on a relief standing behind Darius, and the gate of Xerxes ascribes his success to the Persian god, Ahuramazda.[461]

There is a cuneiform reference to a Mordecai serving as a finance officer in the court of Xerxes at Susa.[462] It is uncertain whether this is the same person who plays such an important role in the book of Esther (see esp. Esther 6:1-2; 8:15; 9:4). However, a German author suggests it must be the same person as it is unlikely that two persons named Mordecai would have served in Xerxes court.[463]

There are three Persian rulers named Artaxerxes. The one related to the Old Testament is probably Aartaxerxes I Longimanus (464-424 B.C.). The Elephantine Papyri mentions him and also mentions Sanballat and Jonathan the high priest. They are referred to in Neh. 2:19 and 12:23.[464]

The governor of the province 'Beyond the River,' Tattenai, is listed with others who sent a letter to Darius opposing the rebuilding of the temple right by Zerubbabel and Jeshua (Ezra 5:2-3). A 502 B.C. Babylonian document mentions Tattenai's name.[465]

Toward the last days of the divided Jewish kingdom simple manufacturing became prominent causing some farmers in Israel and elsewhere to transfer into industry. The Pentateuch gives no instructions regarding manufacturing or in regard to commercial law, but only in regard to farming. This is evidence that these documents were written earlier, prior to this occupational change, not written later during the monarchy or after exile as liberals declare.[466]

As usual critics have found excuses to deny the reliability of Ezra and promote complete uncertainty as to the date of the writings both Ezra and Nehemiah.

Charles C. Torrey and others even assigning Ezra to apocryphal or fraudulent status. [467] However, the discoveries of the Elephantine Papyri and the Jehoiachin tablets makes it possible to *"date Nehemiah in the third quarter of the fifth century with certainty and can locate Ezra with a high degree of confidence shorty after him."*[468]

Despite critics' dismissal of Ezra, the discoveries of early Aramaic writings make the book of Ezra, written partly in Aramaic, seem authentic.[469]

There is evidence from Egyptian papyri from 495 B.C. and later as well as Babylonian documents from various periods, that many of the exiles were prospering in their transplanted cultures.[470] Jewish names have been found on banking records found at Nippor indicating their business activities while in exile.[471] It is thought that many Israelites may have been reluctant to return to Jerusalem at that time because of their success among these other nations.

CONCLUSION

It seems that sufficient evidence has been presented that any truly objective person would acknowledge the Old Testament to be historically reliable. To quote W.F. Albright again, *"There can be no doubt that archaeology has confirmed the substantial historicity of Old Testament tradition."*[472]

Hopefully by now you are seeing that the persons, places, and events recorded in the Old Testament are thoroughly based upon reliable history and that the Old Testament is a book that can be trusted. If you have allowed the evidence to convince you of those facts, it would be reasonable and prudent to consider the Bible's claims to have more than of merely human origin.

A brief Evangelical Christian explanation regarding the origin of the Old Testament is this: The authors were guided by the Spirit of God in their writing and in their selection and use of previously written material (as in Moses' case). This guidance resulted in their original writings being without any errors whether they wrote of earlier times or of their own.

This was not in any sense automatic writing nor with a few exceptions by dictation. Instead, God utilized the unique personality, vocabulary, and style of each individual to communicate precisely what He wished. This would not be difficult for the God who is presented within the pages of the Tanakh.

Finally, it is very significant to recognize these words from Arnold and Beyer's conclusion to their Encountering the Old Testament: *"The Old Testament has no clearly stated completion or resolution. Instead the Old Testament ends in expectation, awaiting a fuller revelation to usher in a new kingdom and its Messiah. The Old Testament's many and varied prophecies about the coming son of David and the new era point to a future time ... 'How are the Old Testament's claims resolved in history?'"* [473] They aren't resolved without the messenger preceding God returning to His Temple (Malachi 3), the revealing of the promised Messiah (Daniel 7:13, 9:25), the fulfillment of the atoning work of Messiah (Isaiah 53) and the establishment of the promised New Covenant Jeremiah (31:33).

Endnotes

[1] That the Old Testament claims Divine origin can be seen by anyone who pays attention to the text when they read it. That alone is insufficient evidence of divine origin but would seem to be a necessary element for consideration. In this regard it is important to realize that the religious scriptures of most religions do not even claim to be from God!

[2] Robert Dick Wilson. Is The Higher Criticism Scholarly? Sunday School Times Company, 1922, 1950. p. 8. Conversation between Wilson and Philip E. Howard

[3] Werner Keller. The Bible As History (trans. By William Neil). William Morrow & Co., 1956. p. 305.

[4] p. 305.

[5] Ibid, p. 10.

[6] Herman Wouk. This Is My God. Doubleday & Company, 1961. p. 191. "We do not have under glass the tablets of stone, nor the book of the law that Deuteronomy says Moses wrote before he died. Too much time has passed. The bulldozers of conquest have leveled and leveled again the temples, the museums, and the archive halls of the Jewish people. Very little was left after the sack of Jerusalem by the Babylonians twenty-five hundred years ago. Nothing was left after Titus razed the holy city again six centuries later. All we have of the Torah of Moses today is very, very late copies, the earliest fragments being less than two thousand years old." This was written over fifty years ago and before knowledge of the more recent manuscripts of the Pentateuch.

[7] John Taylor. "The Five Books." David Alexander & Pat Alexander (Ed.). Eerdman's Handbook to the Bible. GuidePosts, 1973. p. 125.

[8] Clyde T Francisco. Introducing the Old Testament. Broadman Press, 1977. p. 41.

[9] Neil Lightfoot. How We Got Our Bible. Baker Books, 3rd ed., 2003. pp. 24, 212. This "was the time of Ezra, Nehemiah and Malachi" Josephus. Against Apion.I.8. Nothing has been added since Malachi. The Apocrypha were never considered authoritative scripture or part of the canon by the Jews.

[10] John Howard Raven. Old Testament Introduction: General and Special. Fleming H. Revel, 2nd ed., 1910. p. 24.

[11] Ibid.

[12] Examples of writings alleged to be from persons of prominence but excluded from the Hebrew Old Testament because they were fraudulent include: The Wisdom of Solomon, The Letter of Jeremiah, the Prayer of Manasseh, additions to the books of Esther and Daniel. There are many others.

[13] The Bhagadavad Gida is a Hindu writing, written in order to reconcile Buddhism with Hinduism so as to eliminate this competition. It succeeded in eradicating Buddhism in India at that time. It is a story of a fictional hero.

161

[14] C.S. Lewis. "Modern Theology and Biblical Criticism." p. 154. In <u>Christian Reflections</u>. Walter Hooper (Ed.). William B. Eerdmans Publishing, 1967.

[15] Ibid. p. 155.

[16] Robert Dick Wilson. <u>Is The Higher Criticism Scholarly?</u> p. 13.

[17] Steven Masood. <u>The Bible and the Quran; A Question of Integrity.</u>OM Authentic Media, 2001. p. 10.

[18] Bruce M. Metzger "Introduction" <u>The Bible Through the Ages</u>. Readers Digest Association, 1996. p. 13.

[19] Walter C. Kaiser Jr. <u>The Old Testament Documents: Are They Reliable & Relevant?</u> IVP, 2001. p. 58.

[20] W.F. Albright. "Archaeology Confronts Biblical Criticism." <u>The American Scholar</u>. April 1938. p. 86. Referenced in McDowell. <u>New Evidence That Demands a Verdict</u>. p. 432.

[21] A. Rendle Short. <u>Archaeology Gives Evidence</u>, InterVarsity Press, 1951. p. 18.

[22] Walter C. Kaiser Jr. <u>The Old Testament Documents: Are They Reliable & Relevant?</u> pp. 22, 25.

[23] Gerald C. Tilley <u>Defending The Christian Faith.</u> Vol. 1, 2nd ed., 2018. pp. 30, 112, 113.

[24] John Howard Raven. <u>Old Testament Introduction</u>. p. 93.

[25] Ibid. pp. 93-95.

[26] <u>The Bible Through the Ages</u>. Readers Digest Association. 1996. p. 48.

[27] Ibid. pp. 48-49.

[28] See: Deuteronomy 4:15-19, 23-39; 64.

[29] Dewayne Bryant. "The Bible's Buried Secrets." <u>Reason and Revelation.</u> August, 2009. Vol. 29, No. 8. p. 4.

[30] Ibid.

[31] Ibid.

[32] Ibid. Referencing James K. Hoffmeier. <u>Israel in Egypt: The Evidence for the Authenticity of the Exodus Tradition</u>. Oxford University Press, 1996. pp. 83-84.

[33] Ibid. Hoffmeier. p. 109.

[34] Ibid. Hoffmeier. p. 115.

[35] Ibid. Hoffmeier. pp. 165-179.

[36] Ibid, Referencing Egyptologist Kenneth Kitchen. "The Desert Tabernacle: Pure Fiction or Plausible Account?" <u>Bible Review</u>. December, 2000. 16:14-21. & Michael Homan. "The Divine Warrior in His Tent: A Military Model for Yahweh's Tabernacle." <u>Bible Review.</u> December, 2000. 16:22-33.

[37] Ibid. p. 5.

[38] Robert Dick Wilson. <u>Is The Higher Criticism Scholarly?</u> p. 32.

[39] Ibid.

[40] William Henry Green. <u>General Introduction to the Old Testament: The Text</u>. Scribners, 1926. p. 179. Cited by Howard F. Vos. <u>Beginnings in the Old Testament</u>. Moody Press, 1975. p. 16.

[41] Norman L. Geisler & William E. Nix. <u>From God to Us</u>. p. 139.

[42] Ibid.

[43] Gleason Archer. A Survey of Old Testament Introduction. pp. 25-26.

[44] Neil Lightfoot. How We Got Our Bible. pp. 142-143.

[45] John Howard Raven. Old Testament Introduction. p. 71. This is important because many of these interpretations of the Old Testament text show a definite Messianic emphasis that dramatically changed after the ministry of Jesus and Christian emphasis upon His fulfillment of the prophecies.

[46] Neil Lightfoot. How We Got Our Bible. p. 129.

[47] Ibid. pp. 129-130.

[48] Ibid.

[49] Ibid. p. 133. The Talmud is much like an encyclopedia containing Jewish civil and religious law and tradition. It was begun about 300 B.C. or earlier and completed in the 400's A.D.

[50] Ibid. pp. 130-131.

[51] Neil Lightfoot. How We Got Our Bible. pp. 141-147. Norman L. Geisler & William E. Nix. From God to Us. pp. 191-195.

[52] Mark R. Norton. "Texts and Manuscripts of the Old Testament." Philip Wesley Comfort (Ed.). The origin of the Bible. Tyndale House Publishers, 2003. pp. 166-167.

[53] Hershel Shanks, The Mystery and Meaning of the Dead Sea Scrolls. Random House Inc., 1998. p. 17. Note 19. p. 205. (Also, p. 83).

[54] Mark R. Norton. "Texts and Manuscripts of the Old Testament" p. 166.

[55] Hershel Shanks. The Mystery and Meaning of the Dead Sea Scrolls. p. xv.

[56] Randall Price. The Stones Cry Out. Harvest House, 1997. p. 277.

[57] Neil Lightfoot. How We Got Our Bible. p. 135. Randall Price. The Stones Cry Out. p. 284.

[58] Randall Price. The Stones Cry Out. Harvest House, 1997. p. 283.

[59] Andre Dupont-Summer. The Dead Sea Scrolls: A Preliminary Survey. Blackwell, 1952. p. 99. Referenced by Hershel Shanks, The Mystery and Meaning of the Dead Sea Scrolls. pp. xv-xvi.

[60] Hershel Shanks, The Mystery and Meaning of the Dead Sea Scrolls. p. 183. Referencing Allegro's speculation and imagination.

[61] Ibid.

[62] Ibid. p. 196. In 1970 Allegro published a book alleging that Jesus was a fictional character invented by early Christians due to the use of hallucinogenic mushrooms. He wrote that original Christianity was an esoteric hallucinogenic cult. The book was repudiated by prominent British scholars including Allegro's Oxford University mentor. This continued habit of imaginary speculation and distortion of the facts finally destroyed his reputation and his career.

[63] Edmund Wilson. The Scrolls From the Dead Sea. Oxford University Press, 1953. p. 104. Cited by Hershel Shanks, The Mystery and Meaning of the Dead Sea Scrolls. p. xvi.

[64] Hershel Shanks, The Mystery and Meaning of the Dead Sea Scrolls. p. xvii.

[65] Ibid, p. 142.

[66] Gleason Archer. A Survey of Old Testament Introduction. Moody Press, 1974. p. 25.

[67] Ibid. p. 28.

[68] Ibid.

[69] Neil Lightfoot. How We Got Our Bible. p. 28. "… in the middle of Daniel 2:4 the Hebrew stops and the Aramaic begins exactly as our text reads two thousand years later. The Hebrew portion resumes at the end of chapter 7. This transition of Aramaic to Hebrew is also confirmed by the Dead Sea Scrolls. For of the two manuscripts that have this section, both have the change from Aramaic to Hebrew precisely where our modern text has it."

[70] Hershel Shanks. The Mystery and Meaning of the Dead Sea Scrolls. p. 83.

[71] Ibid.

[72] Randall Price. Secrets of the Dead Sea Scrolls. Harvest House Publishers, 1996. p. 145.

[73] Bruce K. Waitke. "Forward." Ellis R. Brotzman Old Testament Textual Criticism. Baker Books, 1994. p. 10.

[74] Randall Price. Secrets of the Dead Sea Scrolls. p. 146.

[75] Hershel Shanks, The Mystery and Meaning of the Dead Sea Scrolls. p. 151. Shanks suggests that, "Each of the world's peoples is allotted a divine son …" He then gives examples of the pagan gods worshipped by Israel's neighbors as if this is the obvious intent of the phrase. Liberals seem unable to resist presenting speculations as support for their rejection of orthodox biblical beliefs.

[76] Bruce Waitke. "Foward" in Ellis Brotzman. Old Testament Textual Criticism. p. 10. Citing Douglas Stuart. "Inerrancy and Textual Criticism" from Roger Nicole and J. Ramsey Michaels (Ed.). Inerrancy and Common Sense. Baker Books, 1980. p. 98.

[77] Gleason Archer. A Survey of Old Testament Introduction. p. 19.

[78] Neil Lightfoot. How We Got Our Bible. p. 138.

[79] Ibid.

[80] Ibid. pp. 138-139.

[81] The Old Testament is translated from the Hebrew text, but our New Testament most often quotes from the Greek Text (LXX) or even paraphrases the O. T. passage. This has frequently caused confusion when comparing the Old Testament reference to the NT and in some cases gives the illusion of a contradiction or discrepancy between them.

[82] Gleason Archer. A Survey of Old Testament Introduction. pp. 21-22.

[83] <answersingenesis.org/moses-documentary-hypothesis>

[84] Ibid.

[85] Dewayne Bryant. "The Bible's Buried Secrets." p. 6.

[86] Walter C. Kaiser Jr. The Old Testament Documents. p. 55. Hermann Gunkel. The Legends of Genesis. Schocken, 1964. p. 1.

[87] Kenneth A. Kitchen. "Some Egyptian Backgrounds to the Old Testament." Tyndale House Bulletins, 1960. No. 5, 6. p. 99. Cited by McDowell The New Evidence That Demands A Verdict. p. 475.

[88] Edwin Yamauchi. Composition and Corroboration in Classical and Biblical Studies. Presbyterian & Reformed Publishing, 1964. pp. 1 1-12.

[89] Merrill, Unger.Archaeology and the Old Testament. Zondervan Publishing Co., 1954. pp. 120-121.

[90] Walter C. Kaiser Jr. The Old Testament Documents. pp. 16-17. Actual source documents may be referred to in Genesis 2:4; 5:1; 6:9; 10:1; 11:27. Inspiration in those cases would mean that God guided Moses in his selection of pre-existing records so that no errors would have been included in the Genesis accounts.

[91] Kenneth A. Kitchen. "Some Egyptian Backgrounds to the Old Testament." Tyndale House Bulletins, 1960. No. 5, 6. p. 99. Cited by McDowell The New Evidence That Demands A Verdict. p. 475.

[92] Ibid.

[93] Ibid.

[94] Ibid.

[95] Josh McDowell. New Evidence That Demands a Verdict. Thomas Nelson, 1999. pp. 391-395.

[96] Bill Arnold & Bryan E. Beyer. Encountering the Old Testament. p. 70.

[97] Gleason Archer. A Survey of Old Testament Introduction. 1974. pp. 84-85. Cited in Josh McDowell. New Evidence That Demands a Verdict. p. 493.

[98] G. Herbert Livingstone. The Pentateuch in Its' Cultural Context. Baker Book House, 1974. p. 227. Cited by McDowell in New Evidence That Demands a Verdict. p. 394.

[99] William F. Albright. The Archaeology of Palestine. Penguin Books, rev. 1960. p. 225.

[100] Dewayne Bryant. "The Bible's Buried Secrets." p. 6. See Eric Lyons "Did God Create Animals or Man First?" 2002. <www.apologeticspress.org/articles/513>

[101] W.F. Albright. "Archaeology Confronts Biblical Criticism." The American Scholar, April, 1938. p. 185. Cited by McDowell. The New Evidence That Demands A Verdict. p. 429.

[102] Herman Wouk. This Is My God. p. 315.

[103] Ibid. p. 319.

[104] Kenneth A. Kitchen. Ancient Orient and the Old Testament. InterVarsity press, 1966. pp. 28-33.

[105] Julius Wellhausen. Prolegomena to the History of Israel. Trans. by Black & Menzies, 1885. pp. 3-4. Originally published in 1878 under the title History of Israel. Cited by Josh McDowell. New Evidence That Demands a Verdict. p. 448.

[106] Richard Elliot Friedman. Who Wrote The Bible? Harper & Row, 1987. p. 26. He could have just said, "I don't know" instead of writing an entire book to reveal that fact.

[107] Richard Elliot Friedman. "Who Wrote the Flood Story?" Adapted from his book, The Bible With Sources Revealed. Harper San Francisco, 2003. Also used on the TV Documentary NOVA: "The Bible's Buried Secrets." <www.pbs.org/wgbh/nova/bible/flood.html>

[108] Ibid.

[109] <www.pbs.org/wgbh/nova/bible/flood.html>

[110] It is not authentic scholarship, to assume a theory to be true, create evidence that appears to substantiate the theory to those without the requisite knowledge to see the deception and then claim the evidence supports the theory. .It is also dishonest to promote a thoroughly disproven theory because it justifies the conclusion you prefer. If you still question the accuracy of the demolition of Wellhausen's Documentary Hypothesis. I suggest you read the thorough evaluation in Josh McDowell's excellent New Evidence That Demands A Verdict. pp. 389-533.

[111] Bill Arnold & Bryan E. Beyer. Encountering the Old Testament. p. 72.

[112] Edwin Yamauchi. Composition and Corroboration in Classical and Biblical Studies. Presbyterian & Reformed Publishing, 1964. pp. 33-35.

[113] When Wellhausen developed his theory relatively little information was available about the ancient Near East so he felt he could speculate freely. Even then, however there was some information that cast doubt upon his speculations. Now a wealth of information is known which reveals the inaccuracies and distortions he relied upon.

[114] Edwin Yamauchi. Composition and Corroboration in Classical and Biblical Studies. p. 30. Referencing Cyrus Gordon. "Higher Critics and Forbidden Fruit." Christianity Today, 4 (November 23, 1959). pp. 131-134.

[115] Ibid. p. 21.

[116] Ibid. pp. 21-22.

[117] Josh McDowell. New Evidence That Demands a Verdict, Thomas Nelson, 1999. pp. 384-385.

[118] Josh McDowell. New Evidence That Demands a Verdict. pp. 385-386.

[119] Ibid. Referencing Gleason Archer. A Survey of Old Testament Introduction. pp. 106-108.

[120] Ibid. Leviticus 16:10; Deut. 23:12-13; Numbers 2:1-31; 10:14-20.

[121] Robert Dick Wilson. Is The Higher Criticism Scholarly? p. 15.

[122] Ibid. p. 68. There are many additional examples that could be cited.

[123] Ibid.

[124] Sanhedrin 21b-22a, also Baba Bathra 14b. Cited by Arnold & Beyer. Encountering the Old Testament. p. 69.

[125] Ibid.

[126] In fact, The New International Version of 1984 translates Genesis 2:19 this way. See also J.H. Hertz. (Ed.) The Pentateuch and Halftorahs. Soncino Press, 2nd ed., 1937. This Jewish translation from the Hebrew reads, "The Lord God, having formed out of the ground every beast of the field and every fowl of heaven, brought them unto the man." Note this authoritatively shows this passage agrees with chapter one. The creatures were created prior to man.

[127] Jason Lisle. "Two Creation Accounts?" Acts & Facts. Institute for Creation Research. September, 2015. p. 13.

[128] Bill Arnold & Bryan E. Beyer. Encountering the Old Testament. Baker Books, 1999. p. 81.

[129] Kenneth C. Davis. Don't Know Much About The Bible. William Morrow and Company, Inc., 1998. p. 51.

[130] For example, Abram is also Abraham, Sarai is Sara, Jacob is also known as Israel. This continued even in New Testament times. Peter was also called Simon and Cephus, Mark was also known as John and Paul mentions a coworker, "Jesus who is called Justus" (Col. 4 :11).

[131] Norman Geisler & Thomas Howe. When Critics Ask. Baker Books, 1992. p. 56.

[132] <cs.umd.edu/-mvz/bible/doc-hyp.pd >

[133] Norman Geisler & Thomas How. When Critics Ask. Baker Books 1992. p. 178.

[134] Steven Masood. The Bible and the Qu'ran: A Question of Integrity, Paternoster Publishing, 2001. p. 10.

[135] Richard Elliot Friedman. "Who Wrote the Flood Story?" Also utilized On NOVA: "The Bible's Buried Secrets."

[136] John Howard Raven. Old Testament Introduction, p. 95.

[137] Ibid. pp. 95-98.

[138] Gleason L. Archer. A Survey of Old Testament Introduction. Moody Press, 1964. p. 101. Cited in New Evidence That Demands a Verdict. pp. 385-386.

[139] Robert Dick Wilson. Which Bible? David Otis Fuller (Ed.). p. 42. Cited by Josh McDowell. The New Evidence That Demands A Verdict. p. 12.

[140] C.H. Kang & Ethel R. Nelson. The Discovery of Genesis. Concordia Publishing House, 1979. pp. ix, xiv, xvii. Ethel R. Nelson & Richard E. Broadberry. The Mystery Confucius Couldn't Solve. Concordia Publishing House, 1994. pp. 9-10, 19-20ff.

[141] W.F. Albright. Stone Age to Christianity. John Hopkins Press, 1940. pp. 213-217.

[142] W.F. Albright. The Biblical Period From Abraham to Ezra: an historical survey. Harper & Row Publishers. Revised, 1960. p. 5.

[143] Randall Price. The Stones Cry Out. p. 92.

[144] Ibid. p. 93.

[145] J.A. Thompson. The Ancient Near Eastern Treaties and the Old Testament. The Tyndale Press, 1964. p. 7. See also, p. 21.

[146] Ibid.

[147] Donald E. Demaray. Bible Study Source-Book. Zondervan Publishing House, 1964, p. 237.

[148] J. Kenneth Eakins & Jack P. Lewis. "Archaeology and Biblical Study." Trent C. Butler (Ed.). Holman Bible Dictionary. Holman Bible publishers, 1991. p. 89.

[149] Richard Purtill. Thinking About Religion. A philosophical Introduction to Religion. Prentice-Hall Inc., 1978. pp. 84-85.

[150] Ibid. p. 85.

[151] Werner Keller. The Bible As History. pp. 99-100. Also, Josh McDowell. New Evidence That Demands a Verdict. pp. 11, 47.

[152] W.F. Albright. The Archaeology of Palestine and the Bible. Revel, 1933. p. 142. Cited in McDowell. New Evidence That Demands a Verdict. p. 446.

153 A. Rendle Short. <u>Archaeology Gives Evidence.</u> pp. 21-22. Josh McDowell. <u>New Evidence That Demands a Verdict.</u> pp. 444-447. McDowell quotes Albright's change of mind due to his discoveries and other scholars' conclusions.

154 John H. Walton. Victor H. Mathews & Mark W. Chavalas. <u>Bible Background Commentary - Old Testament</u>. InterVarsity Press, 2000. pp. 45-47.

155 <www.biblehistory.net/newsletter/chedorlamomer.htm> Referencing British Museum documents: BM35404, BM34062, BM35496.

156 W.F. Albright. <u>The Biblical Period From Abraham To Ezra</u>. Harper & Row, 1963. pp. 3, 6.

157 Nigel Stillman. "History: Battles of Hamarabi,Part One The Rise of Babylon." <www.warlordgames.com/history-battles -of-hamarabi-part-one-the-rise-of-babylon?> Citing the tablets of ancient Mari.

158 W.F. Albright. <u>Archaeology and the Religion of Israel</u>. John Hopkins Press, 1942. p. 176. History, Archaeology and Christian Humanism. McGraw Hill, 1964.

159 D. James Kennedy & Jerry Newcombe. <u>What If The Bible Had Never Been Written?</u> Thomas Nelson, 1998. p. 216.

160 Nelson Glueck. <u>Rivers in the Desert</u>. Farrar, Straus, & Cadahy, 1958. p. 31. Cited by Josh McDowell <u>New Evidence That Demands a Verdict</u>. p. 61.

161 James L. Kelso. "The Archaeology of the Bible." <u>Holman Study Bible, Revised Standard Version</u>. A.J. Holman Co., 1962. p. 1198.

162 Randall Price. <u>The Stones Cry Out</u>. pp. 167-170. <u>The Bible Through the Ages</u>. p. 56.

163 Randall Price. <u>The Stones Cry Out</u>. p. 169.

164 "The Balaam Inscription." <u>Truth Magazine</u>. Daniel H. King. pp. 556-557. September 8, 1977. <www.truthmagazine.com/archives/vol.21>

165 Ibid.

166 Ibid.

167 Josh McDowell. <u>The New Evidence That Demands A Vierdict. p. 61.</u> Citing: W.F. Albright. <u>The Archaeology of Palestine</u>. 1960. pp. 127-128.

168 An example was the recent "Lost Tomb of Jesus" film on the Discovery Channel in 2007 and book by the same name. This has been thoroughly repudiated by both historians and archaeologists including the archaeologists who made the alleged tomb discovery. One reason for dismissing the claims that it was the tomb of Jesus and his family was that Jesus, Joseph and Mary were three of the most common names in first century Israel. The author of the book admitted many of the associations made "were speculative." For example, Jesus was never called the "son of Joseph" by his followers as designated on the burial box. (ossuary). See the internet analysis of this issue by Ben Witherington at: <benwitherington.blogspot.com/2007/02-jesus-tomb-titannic>

169 Josh McDowell. <u>New Evidence That Demands A Verdict.</u> p. 91.

170 Ibid.

171 J. Kenneth Eakins & Jack P. Lewis. "Archaeology and Biblical Study." p. 83.

172 Ibid. p. 84.

173 Ibid. p. 85.

174 Ibid. pp. 84, 86.

175 Ibid. p. 85.

176 Randall Price. The Stones Cry Out. p. 25.

177 Clifford A. Wilson. "Does Archaeology Prove The Bible?" Bible & Spade. Winter, 1972. Vol. 1, No. 1. p. 7.

178 Ibid. pp. 332-333. Interview with Keith Schoville, November 19, 1996.

179 Ibid. p. 39. See quote from Interview with archaeologist Bryant Wood. November 1996 on that page.

180 J. Kenneth Eakins & Jack P. Lewis. "Archaeology and Biblical Study." p. 87. See the New King James, Updated New American Standard & New International Versions for the improved translations.

181 Clifford A. Wilson. "Does Archaeology Prove The Bible?" Bible & Spade. p. 5.

182 Bill Arnold & Bryan E. Beyer. Encountering the Old Testament. pp. 286-287.

183 Ibid.

184 Ibid. p. 287. Ugaritic poetry portrays polytheism, whereas Hebrew poetry exalts and worships the one true God.

185 Ibid. p. 91.

186 Ibid. pp. 88-89.

187 Ibid. p. 89.

188 Ibid.

189 Ibid. p. 90.

190 Randall Price. The Stones Cry Out. p. 25. Gonzalo Baez-Camargo. Archaeological Commentary on the Bible. Doubleday & Company, Inc., 1984. p. xxii.

191 J. Kenneth Eakins & Jack P. Lewis. "Archaeology and Biblical Study." p. 91.

192 Donald J. Wiseman. "The Bottleneck of Archaeological Publication." Biblical Archaeology Review. September/October 1990. Vol. XVI, No. 5. p. 61.

193 Randall Price. The Stones Cry Out. p. 44. Interview with Amihai Mazar, Institute of Archaeology, Jerusalem. October, 1996.

194 Ibid. pp. 45-47. Referencing Edwin Yamauchi. The Stones and the Scriptures. Baker Books, 1981.

195 Ibid. p. 46.

196 Kenneth A. Kitchen. On the Reliability of the Old Testament. Eerdman's Publishing, 2003. p. 183.

197 Randall Price. The Stones Cry Out. pp. 45-47. Referencing Edwin Yamauchi. The Stones and the Scriptures. Baker Books, 1981.

198 Dewayne Bryant. "The Bible's Buried Secrets." p. 4.

199 Randall Price. The Stones Cry Out. pp. 35-36. Interview with Amihai Mazar, Institute of Archaeology, Jerusalem. October, 1996.

169

[200] Robert Dick Wilson. Is The Higher Criticism Scholarly? pp. 20-21.
[201] Ibid. "Shishak, Zerah, So, Tirhakeh, Necho and Hophra, kings of Cush and Egypt; 5-Pileser, Shalmaneser, Sargon, Sennacherib, and Esarhaddon, kings of Assyria; Merodach-Baladan, Nebuchadnezzar, Evil-Merodach and Belshazzar, kings of Babylon; and Cyrus, Darius Xerxes, and Artaxerxes kings of Persia, all appear in the scriptures in their correct order as attested by their own records or by other contemporaneous evidence. The same is true, also, of the kings of Damascus, Tyre and Moab." Wilson is showing the inconsistency of critics, who despite the known errors of secular historians in regard to the rulers of these empires, those historians are still valued as reliable. Yet the critics reject the accuracy of the Old Testament which has avoided those errors.
[202] Ibid. pp. 38-39.
[203] Millar Burrows. What Mean These Stones? Meridian Books, 1957. p. 291. Cited by McDowell. New Evidence That Demands a Verdict. pp. 61-62.
[204] William Foxwell Albright. The Archaeology of Palestine. Penguin Books, 1960. pp. 127-128. Cited by McDowell. New Evidence That Demands a Verdict. p. 61.
[205] Millar Burrows, Cited from Howard Vos. Can I Trust the Bible? Moody Press, 1963. p. 176. McDowell. New Evidence That Demands a Verdict. p. 62.
[206] Raymond Bowman. "Old Testament Research Between the Great Wars" In The Study of the Bible Today and Tomorrow. Harold H. Willoughby (Ed.). University of Chicago Press, 1947. p. 30. Cited by McDowell. New Evidence That Demands a Verdict. p. 100.
[207] Peter Farb. The Land, Wildlife and Peoples of the Bible. p. 154.
[208] Ibid.
[209] Ibid.
[210] Personal conversation between Dr. Earl Radmacher and Josh McDowell on Radmacher's attending Dr. Gleuck's lecture in Dallas. Reported in McDowell. New Evidence That Demands a Verdict. pp. 11-12.
[211] Randall Price. The Stones Cry Out. pp. 60-62.
[212] Brian Thomas. "Modern Archaeology and Genesis." Acts & Facts. January, 2016. Vol. 45, No. 1. p. 16. Citing from C. Davis. Dating the Old Testament. RJ Communications, 2007. p. 93.
[213] Robert Dick Wilson. Is The Higher Criticism Scholarly? p. 14. Wilson refers to King, The Seven Tablets of Creation and Jensen Assyrisch-Babylonische Mythen und Epen.
[214] A.R. Millard. "A New Babylonian 'Genesis Story." Tyndale Bulletin 18, 1967. pp. 17-18. Cited by Randall Price. The Stones Cry Out. p. 70.
[215] Bill Arnold & Bryan E. Beyer. Encountering the Old Testament. p. 78.

[216] Brian Thomas. "Modern Archaeology and Genesis." p. 16. Citing B. Cooper <u>Authenticity of the Book of Genesis</u>. Creation Science Movement, 2012. p. 53. Cylinder seals were images, or words or both carved in reverse on a cylinder which was then rolled across soft clay to form an image. These were used by Sumerians, Akkadians, Hittites, and Syrians to create permanent records. See: <ancientcode.com/the-mark-of-history-the-incredible-ancient-sumerian-cylinder-seals/>

[217] See: John D. Morris. "Traditions of a Global Flood." <u>Acts & Facts</u>. November, 2014. Vol. 43, No. 11. p. 15.

[218] Bryant G. Wood. (Ed.). Bible and Spade. Vol. 1, No. 1. pp. 19-20. Referencing William W. Hallo. "Antediluvian Cities." <u>Journal of Cuneiform Studies</u>. Vol. XXIII, No. 3. October 1970.

[219] Ibid.

[220] Ibid. p. 90.

[221] Werner Keller. <u>The Bible as History</u>. pp. 99-102. Howard Vos. <u>Genesis and Archaeology</u>. p. 53.

[222] Randall Price. <u>The Stones Cry Out</u>. p. 92.

[223] William Foxwell Albright. <u>The Biblical Period From Abraham to Ezra</u>. Harper & Row, 1960. p. 3.

[224] Ibid. p. 2.

[225] Clyde T Francisco. <u>Introducing the Old Testament</u>. p. 69.

[226] Ibid.

[227] Peter Farb. <u>The Land, Wildlife and Peoples of the Bible</u>. pp. 28-29.

[228] James L. Kelso. "The Archaeology of the Bible." p. 1196.

[229] W.F. Albright. <u>The Biblical Period From Abraham to Ezra</u>. Harper & Row, 1960. p. 2.

[230] Ibid. p. 6. Referencing <u>Bulletin American School of Oriental Research</u>, No. 163. pp. 44-48.

[231] Peter Farb. <u>The Land, Wildlife and Peoples of the Bible</u>. p. 157.

[232] Ibid.

[233] Ibid. pp. 37-38.

[234] Clifford A. Wilson. "Does Archaeology Prove The Bible?" p. 6.

[235] J. Kenneth Eakins & Jack P. Lewis. "Archaeology and Biblical Study." pp. 91-92.

[236] Clifford A. Wilson. "Does Archaeology Prove The Bible?" p. 6.

[237] Howard F. Vos. <u>Genesis and Archaeology</u>. p. 65.

[238] Peter Farb. <u>The Land, Wildlife and Peoples of the Bible</u>. p. 32.

[239] Howard F. Vos. <u>Genesis and Archaeology</u>. p. 65.

[240] Ibid. pp. 65-66.

[241] W.F. Albright. <u>The Biblical Period From Abraham to Ezra</u>. p. 41.

[242] J. Kenneth Eakins & Jack P. Lewis. "Archaeology and Biblical Study." p. 92.

[243] Randall Price. <u>The Stones Cry Out</u>. pp. 102-104.

[244] Nahum Sarna. "The Patriarchs." in <u>Genesis: World of Myths and Patriarchs.</u> (Ed.) Ada Feyerick. New York University Press, 1996. "As a whole, the patriarchal narratives possess a distinctive flavor unparalleled in the rest of the Bible. They reflect a pattern of living and several socio-legal institutions that are particular to the period but often attested in Near Eastern documents … the antiquity of the Genesis traditions is confirmed by several patriarchal practices that directly contradict the social mores and norms of a later age…" Cited by Randall Price. <u>The Stones Cry Out</u>. p. 92.

[245] Donald E. Demaray. <u>Bible Study Source-Book</u>. p. 236.

[246] Clifford A. Wilson. "Does Archaeology Prove The Bible?" p. 736.

[247] Ibid.

[248] Bill Arnold & Bryan E. Beyer. <u>Encountering the Old Testament</u>. p. 91.

[249] Randall Price. <u>The Stones Cry Out</u>. p. 110.

[250] Ibid. pp. 110-112, 409 notes. First century A.D. historian Josephus and Philo a century earlier wrote extensively about Sodom & Gomorrah. There are also frequent references in extra-biblical writings from Qumran and the apocrypha. See Price p. 409 for specific examples.

[251] Ibid. p. 114.

[252] Ibid. pp. 113-115.

[253] Ibid. pp. 115-118.

[254] Ibid. pp. 117-118.

[255] Ibid. pp. 114-119.

[256] John D. Morris. "Have Sodom and Gomorrah Been Discovered?" <u>Acts & Facts</u>. April 2013. Vol. 42, No. 4. p. 15.

[257] Ibid.

[258] Clifford Wilson. The Impact of Elba on Bible Records. Word of Truth Productions, 1977. pp. 26, 29.

[259] Randall Price. <u>The Stones Cry Out</u>. pp. 114-119.

[260] Eckart Frahm. "Surprising Parallels Between Joseph and King Esarhaddon." <u>Biblical Archaeology Review</u>. May/Jun 2016. Vol. 42, No. 3. p. 49.

[261] Ibid. p. 50.

[262] Examples that appear to refer to previous writings are: Gen. 2:4; 5:1; 6:9; 10:1, etc.

[263] Edwin Yamauchi. <u>Composition and Corroboration in Classical and Biblical Studies</u>. p. 22.

[264] Clifford A. Wilson. "Does Archaeology Prove the Bible?" <u>Bible and Spade</u>. Vol. 1, No. 1. p. 7.

[265] Ibid.

[266] Edwin Yamauchi. <u>Composition and Corroboration in Classical and Biblical Studies</u>. p. 8. Referencing W.A. Ward "The Egyptian Office of Joseph." <u>Journal of Semitic Studies</u>, 5 (1960). pp. 144-145.

[267] Eckart Frahm. "Surprising Parallels Between Joseph and King Esarhaddon." <u>Biblical Archaeology Review</u>. May/Jun 2016. Vol. 42, No. 3. p. 49.

[268] Ibid. pp. 49, 63.

[269] Other sources such as <u>Egypt Today</u> give the date of the inscription as 250 B.C. <www.egypttoday.com/article/4/54056/famine-stela-A-piece -of-Pharoahic-diary>
The Famine Stele was discovered in 1889 by American Egyptologist Charles Wilbour and deciphered first by German Egyptologist Heinrich Brugsch in 1891. This island has many rocks inscribed with writings from different individuals and eras.

[270] Ibid.

[271] Bill Arnold & Bryan E. Beyer. <u>Encountering the Old Testament</u>. p. 47.

[272] <u>The Bible Through the Ages</u>. p. 37.

[273] Ibid.

[274] James L. Kelso. "The Archaeology of the Bible." p. 1197.

[275] Dewayne Bryant. "The Bible's Buried Secrets." p. 4.

[276] Some of the earliest verses suggesting or declaring the oneness of God: Exodus 8:10; 9:14; 19:5; 20:1-5; Deuteronomy 4:35, 39; 32:39;33:26; Joshua 2:11.

[277] W.F. Albright. <u>The Biblical Period From Abraham to Ezra</u>. pp. 22-23. It is quite significant that even such a small detail confirms the accuracy of the Bible.

[278] Eckart Frahm. "Surprising Parallels Between Joseph and King Esarhaddon." p. 63. See Joshua J. Mark. "The Legend of Sargon of Akkad." <u>Ancient History Encyclopedia</u> August, 2014. <www.ancient.eu/article/746/the-legend-of-sargon-of-akkad/>

[279] <www.ancient.eu/article/746/the-legend-of-sargon-of-akkad/> Cited from O.R. Gurney. "The Cuthaean Legend of Naram-sin." <u>Anatolian Studies</u>. The Sultantepe Tablets. Vol. 5, 1995. p. 93.

[280] Peter Farb. <u>The Land, Wildlife and Peoples of the Bible</u>. p. 58.

[281] Bryant G. Wood. "Recent Research on the Date and Setting of the Exodus." Bible And Spade. Fall 2008.

[282] Eugene Merril. <u>Kingdom of Priests</u>. Baker Book House, 1987. p. 57. Cited by Randall Price. <u>The Stones Cry Out</u>. p. 130.

[283] John I. Durham. <u>Exodus</u>. Word Books, 1987. p. xxiii. Cited by Randall Price. <u>The Stones Cry Out</u>. p. 130.

[284] John Taylor. "The Five Books." p. 125.

[285] Ibid. The defeat of the gods of Egypt is revealed in the Nile turning to blood for seven days revealed the powerlessness of the Nile. The darkness for three days revealed the ineptness of the gods of the solar disc and of sunshine and the goddesses of the sky and moon. Destruction of vegetation overthrew the god of crop cycles, etc.

[286] Bill Arnold & Bryan E. Beyer. <u>Encountering the Old Testament</u>. p. 108.

[287] Randall Price. <u>The Stones Cry Out</u>. pp. 208-209.

[288] Ibid. p. 209. It is sometimes explained that God often accommodated His revelation and plans to known and accepted cultural practices but with more significant and unique meaning than that of the pagan usage.

[289] Ibid.

290 Ibid. pp. 1-2. From. "The Stele of Merneptah." William W. Hallo & K. Lawson Younger (Ed.). The Context of Scripture. Brill, 2000. Trans by James K. Hoffmeier.

291 Ibid.

292 James K. Hoffmeier. "Israel in Egypt: The Archaeological Context of the Exodus." Biblical Archaeological Review. Jan/Feb 2007. Vol. 33, No. 1.

293 Ibid.

294 James K. Hoffmeier. Israel in Egypt: The Evidence for the Authenticity of the Exodus Tradition. Oxford University Press, 1996. p. viii.

295 Simcha Jacobovici. "The Exodus Decoded." Documentary on History International. Randall Price. The Stones Cry Out. p. 411. n. 29.

296 Randall Price. The Stones Cry Out. pp. 133, 411. n. 28.

297 Ibid. pp. 411-412. n. 29-34.

298 Ibid. pp. 134, 412. n. 36-38.

299 Manfred Bietak. "Israelites Found In Egypt." Biblical Archaeology Review. Sept/Oct 2003. <baslibrary.org/biblical-archaeology-review/29/5/9>

300 <www.ancientorigins.net/history> The document is catalogued as Lieden 344. It is deteriorated at both ends. The back of the document contains hymns to the Egyptian god Amun, which further establishes its authenticity.

301 Randall Price. The Stones Cry Out. pp. 137-138.

302 Ibid. pp. 134-136.

303 Ibid. p. 132.

304 Simcha Jacobovici. "The Exodus Decoded."

305 Ibid.

306 Peter Farb. The Land, Wildlife and Peoples of the Bible. pp. 66-67.

307 W.F. Albright. The Biblical Period From Abraham to Ezra. p. 22.

308 Ibid. Citing R.H. Pfeiffer. Introduction to the Old Testament (1941). p. 281.

309 Peter Farb. The Land, Wildlife and Peoples of the Bible. p. 84.

310 Bill Arnold & Bryan E. Beyer. Encountering the Old Testament. p. 169.

311 Ibid.

312 Jack P. Lewis. Archaeological Backgrounds to Bible People. Baker Books, 1971. pp. 14-15.

313 Ibid. p. 15. Also, Dewayne Bryant. "The Bible's Buried Secrets." Reason and Revelation. August 2009. Vol. 29, No. 8. pp. 1-2.

314 Manfred Bietak. "Exodus Evidence: An Egyptologist Looks at Biblical History." Biblical Archaeology Review. May/June 2016. Vol. 42, No. 3. p. 32.

315 Dewayne Bryant. "The Bible's Buried Secrets." p. 2.

316 Ibid.

317 Ibid.

318 Ibid. p. 3.

319 Randall Price. The Stones Cry Out. p. 38.

320 W.F. Albright. The Biblical Period From Abraham to Ezra. pp. 39, 42.

321 Ibid. pp. 42, 48.

[322] Ibid. pp. 42-43.

[323] Ibid. pp. 43-44.

[324] Bryant G. Wood. "Did the Israelites Conquer Jericho? A New Look At the Archaeological Evidence." Biblical Archaeology Review. March/April 1990. Vol. XVI, No. 2. pp. 45-46. The author adds that this date 1400 B.C. is 150-200 years earlier than liberal scholars think that Israelites were in Canaan though it seems to fit the evidence and biblical narrative. This major article, (pages 44-59) reestablishes the historical credibility of the destruction of Jericho by the Israelites as presented in the Old Testament book of Joshua.

[325] Ibid. p. 49.

[326] Ibid.

[327] Ibid. p. 46.

[328] Ibid.

[329] Ibid. p. 50.

[330] Ibid. pp. 49-50.

[331] Ibid, pp. 52-53.

[332] Ibid, p. 51.

[333] Plotr Bienkowski. "Jericho Was Destroyed in the Middle Bronze Age, Not the Late Bronze Age." & Bryan G. Wood. "Dating Jericho's Destruction: Bienkowski is Wrong on All Counts." Biblical Archaeology Review. September/October 1990. Vol. XVI, No. 5. pp. 45-49, 68-69. The article by Bienkowski attacked each of four major arguments of Bryant Wood in the March/April, 1990 issue and defended Kathleen Kenyon's date of 1550 B.C. for Jericho's destruction. Parallel to Bienkowski's article was the refutation of Bienkowski's arguments and more detailed data by Wood. Wood seems to have substantiated his dating of approximately 1400 B.C. for the destruction, as well as refuting Bienkowski's arguments for the earlier date. The 1400 B.C. date, along with specific examples cited in the text supports the Biblical account in Joshua.

[334] W.F. Albright. The Biblical Period From Abraham to Ezra. p. 50.

[335] Clifford A. Wilson. "The Bible Was Right After All." Bible & Spade. p. 11.

[336] Dewayne Bryant. "The Bible's Buried Secrets. p. 3.

[337] Kathleen Kenyon. The Bible and Recent Archaeology. John Knox Press, 1987. p. 85. Revised edition. P.R.S. Moorey. Cited by Randall Price. The Stones Cry Out. p. 162.

[338] Randall Price. The Stones Cry Out. p. 167.

[339] Dewayne Bryant. "The Bible's Buried Secrets. p. 3.

[340] Randall Price. The Stones Cry Out. pp. 165-167, 169-170.

[341] Ibid. p. 170.

[342] Randall Price. The Stones Cry Out. p. 169.

[343] Dewayne Bryant. "The Bible's Buried Secrets. p. 3. Historian Philip Davies distorted mistranslations of the inscription as "'house of uncle' and 'house of kettle' was even lampooned in an issue of Biblical Archaeology Review" 1995. Vol. 21, No. 2. See also, Randall Price. The Stones Cry Out. p. 170.

[344] Ibid. p. 4. Quoting Israel Finkelstein speaking on NOVA's two-hour documentary, "The Bible's Buried Secrets" which originally aired in 2008.

[345] Ibid.

[346] Ibid.

[347] Randall Price. The Stones Cry Out. p. 171.

[348] Ibid. pp. 171-172.

[349] Ibid. p. 173.

[350] W.F. Albright. The Biblical Period From Abraham to Ezra. pp. 54-55.

[351] Ibid. p. 54.

[352] Bryant G. Wood. Bible and Spade. Winter 1972. Vol. 1, No. 1. Cover & P.L. Jeroboam II ruled as the Northern Kingdom's 14th king 787-747 B.C.

[353] Jack P. Lewis. Archaeological Backgrounds to Bible People. pp. 99-100. S. Yeivin. "The Date of the Seal Belonging to Shema (the Servant of Jeroboam)." Journal of Near Eastern Studies. XIX (1960). pp. 205-212. Paleography is the deciphering and dating of ancient writing and inscriptions.

[354] Randall Price. The Stones Cry Out. pp. 228-229. Clifford A. Wilson. "The Bible Was Right After All." Bible & Spade. p. 17.

[355] Ibid.

[356] Ibid. p. 230. Price's interview with Amihai Mazar,at the Hebrew University Institute of Archaeology, October 26, 1996.

[357] W.F. Albright. The Biblical Period From Abraham to Ezra. p. 67.

[358] J. Kenneth Eakins & Jack P. Lewis. "Archaeology and Biblical Study." p. 85.

[359] Jack P. Lewis. Archaeological Backgrounds to Bible People. p. 96. J.B. Prichard. (ed.) Ancient Near Eastern Texts Related to the Old Testament. p. 279.

[360] Ibid.

[361] W.F. Albright. The Biblical Period From Abraham to Ezra. p. 67.

[362] Ibid. p. 64.

[363] Hugh Tobias. "Tirzah." Homan Bible Dictionary. p. 1352.

[364] Jack P. Lewis. Archaeological Backgrounds to Bible People. pp. 61-63.

[365] J. Kenneth Eakins & Jack P. Lewis. "Archaeology and Biblical Study." p. 84.

[366] Ibid. p. 65. See: Levi della Vida & W.F. Albright. Bulletin of the American School of Oreintal Research No. 90. pp. 30ff.

[367] Jack P. Lewis. Archaeological Backgrounds to Bible People. pp. 66-67. W.F. Albright argued for two in G. Levi, Della Vida & W.F. Albright. "Some Notes on the Stele of Ben-Hadad." Bulletin of American School of Oriental Research. No. 90 (1943). pp. 30-34. See: M.F. Unger. Israel and the Arameans of Damascus. James Clarke & Co., 1957. pp. 60-81.

[368] Ibid. pp. 68-69. Referencing J. B. Prichard. (Ed.). Ancient Near Eastern Texts Related to the Old Testament. p. 280.

[369] Ibid. p. 69. Referencing Prichard, p. 280 & D.D. Luckenbill. Ancient Records of Assyria and Babylon. University of Chicago Press, 1926. Vol. 1, No. 663.

[370] Ibid. p. 97. See Prichard, p. 281 & A.H. Layard. Nineveh and its Remains. John Murray, 1849, I, pp. 346-348. & R. D. Barnett Illustrations of Old Testament History. The British Museum, 1966. p. 46.

[371] Ibid. J.B. Prichard. (Ed.). Ancient Near Eastern Texts Related to the Old Testament. p. 280.

[372] Ibid. Including Prichard. p. 655.

[373] Ibid. p. 98. Including Prichard. Also, Stephanie Page. "A Stella of Adad-Nirari and Nergal-Eres from Tell al Rima." Iraq. XXX (1968). pp. 139-153. & D.J. Wiseman. "Old Testament Evidence." Christianity Today. XIII (January 3, 1969). p. 319.

[374] Ibid. Referencing Prichard, p. 283.

[375] Ibid. p. 71. D.D. Luckenbill. Ancient Records of Assyria and Babylon. Vol. I, No. 776. See also: Prichard, p. 283.

[376] Randall Price. The Stones Cry Out. pp. 230-231.

[377] W.F. Albright. The Biblical Period From Abraham to Ezra. p. 74. Bulletin of the American School of Oriental Research. No. 149. pp. 53ff.

[378] Ibid. p. 77.

[379] Kenneth A. Kitchen. On the Reliability of the Old Testament. p. 40. See H. Tadmor JCS. Vol. 12 (1958). pp. 79-80, 92-96.

[380] W.F. Albright. The Biblical Period From Abraham to Ezra. p. 74.

[381] Ibid. p. 78.

[382] Randall Price. The Stones Cry Out. pp. 231-232.

[383] Ibid.

[384] Ibid. p. 80. See M. Noth. History of Israel. pp. 271ff. & Albrecht Alt Zeit fur die altestamentliche. Wiss, 1927. pp. 59-81.

[385] Kenneth A. Kitchen. On the Reliability of the Old Testament. p. 43. Referencing D.J. Wiseman. Chronicles of the Chaldean Kings. pp. 19-37, 46-48.

[386] Jack P. Lewis. Archaeological Backgrounds to Bible People. pp. 17-18.

[387] J. Kenneth Eakins & Jack P. Lewis. "Archaeology and Biblical Study." p. 90.

[388] W.F. Albright. The Biblical Period From Abraham to Ezra. p. 59.

[389] Jack P. Lewis. Archaeological Backgrounds to Bible People. pp. 22-23.

[390] Ibid. p. 27. From The Antiquities. x. 5 (1974).

[391] Ibid. pp. 33-34. Referencing J.B. Pritchard (Ed). Ancient Near Eastern Texts Related to the Old Testament, 3rd ed. Princeton University Press, 1954. pp. 282-284.

[392] Jack P. Lewis. Archaeological Backgrounds to Bible People. p. 36.

[393] Ibid. pp. 36-37.

[394] Ibid. pp. 38-39. Citing J.B. Pritchard. Ancient Near Eastern Texts Related to the Old Testament. p. 272.

[395] Clifford A. Wilson. "The Bible Was Right After All." Bible & Spade. Vol. 1, No. 1. (1972). p. 8.

[396] J. Kenneth Eakins & Jack P. Lewis. "Archaeology and Biblical Study." p. 90. See also Clifford A. Wilson. "The Bible Was Right After All." p. 8.

[397] Howard F. Vos. Beginnings in the Old Testament. p. 18. See also Jack P. Lewis. Archaeological Backgrounds to Bible People. pp. 39-40. Sargon's Annals recount his military exploits and a life size relief of him was found at Khorsabad.

[398] Jack P. Lewis. Archaeological Backgrounds to Bible People. pp. 44-46.

[399] Randall Price. The Stones Cry Out. p. 273.

[400] Ibid. pp. 46-47.

[401] Ibid. p. 48. D.W. Thomas. Documents From Old Testament Times. Nelson, 1958. p. 72.

[402] Ibid. pp. 49-50. Referencing D.J. Wiseman. "The Vassal Treaties of Esarhaddon." Iraq. XX, 1 (1958). pp. 1-27.

[403] Ibid. p. 52. Referencing C.J. Gadd. "The Harran Inscriptions of Nabonidus." Anatolian Studies, VIII (1958). pp. 69-72. & J.B. Pritchard. Ancient Near Eastern Texts Related to the Old Testament. p. 294.

[404] Ibid. p. 52. J.B. Pritchard. Ancient Near Eastern Texts Related to the Old Testament. p. 294.

[405] Ibid. p. 52.

[406] Randall Price. The Stones Cry Out. pp. 252-253.

[407] Ibid. p. 253.

[408] Randall Price. The Stones Cry Out. pp. 79-80.

[409] J. Kenneth Eakins & Jack P. Lewis. "Archaeology and Biblical Study." p. 84.

[410] Ibid. pp. 73-76. R.W. Rogers. Cuneiform Parallels to the Old Testament. Abingdon Press, 1926. pp. 210ff. Also, J.A. Brinkman. "Merodach-baladan II" Studies Presented to H. Leo Oppenheim. University of Chicago, 1964. pp. 6-53.

[411] Ibid. pp. 73-74. Josephus. Antiquities of the Jews. x.2.2. pp. 30ff.

[412] Donald J. Wiseman. "The Bottleneck of Archaeological Publication." Biblical Archaeology Review. September/October 1990. p. 61.

[413] Ibid.

[414] Randall Price. The Stones Cry Out. pp. 234-235.

[415] Ibid.

[416] Jack P. Lewis. Archaeological Backgrounds to Bible People. pp. 27-28.

[417] Ibid. pp. 29-32. Citing Herodotus. Histories. ii. p. 161. Serculus Diodorus. Library of History i.68. pp. 1-5.

[418] Jack P. Lewis. Archaeological Backgrounds to Bible People. pp. 29-32. Both Egyptian and Greeks authors refer to Hophra and his palace has been found in Memphis, Egypt.

[419] Clifford A. Wilson. "The Bible Was Right After All." Bible & Spade. p. 9.

[420] Ibid. p. 76.

[421] Ibid. p. 77.

[422] Ibid. p. 81. See D.J. Wiseman. Illustrations from Bibliical Archaeology. Tyndale Press, 1958. p. 71. & Steven Langdon. Building Inscriptions of the Neo-Babylonian Empire. Ernest LeRoux, 1905. pp. 61-63, 81-83.

[423] Ibid. p. 84. Josephus. Antiquities of the Jews. x,11.1. p. 228. Another ancient document, Codex Laurentianus, states the siege was three years.

[424] Randall Price. The Stones Cry Out. pp. 254-255.

[425] Ibid.

[426] Jack P. Lewis. Archaeological Backgrounds to Bible People. pp. 85-86. J.B. Pritchard. (Ed.). Ancient Near Eastern Texts Related to the Old Testament. p. 309.

[427] Ibid. p. 86. D.J. Wiseman. Chronicles of Chaldean Kings. p. 38.

[428] Ibid, D.J. Wiseman. Chronicles of Chaldean Kings. p. 38.

[429] Edwin Yamauchi. Composition and Corroboration on Classical and Biblical Studies. p. 24.

[430] Even that late date could not explain the prophecy concerning the coming of the Messiah so they had to come up with some way to obscure that aspect of the document.

[431] Edwin Yamauchi. Composition and Corroboration on Classical and Biblical Studies. p. 24.

[432] Clifford A. Wilson. "The Bible Was Right After All." Bible & Spade. pp. 9-10. We now have tablets held at Yale University recording administrative matters handled by Belshazzar as acting regent or king.

[433] <www.brittanica.com/biography/Nabonidus> & <www.newworldencyclopedia.org/entry/Nabonidus> Xemophonn informs of the killing of the young ruler of Babylon without mentioning his name. The Nabonidus cylinders found at Sipper and Ur. Mention Belshazzar as his son and co-regent. A stone carved relief pictures Nabonidus worshipping the sun, Venus and the moon-god, Allah. These are all made by 540 B.C. or before.

[434] Ibid. See: Sidney S. Smith. Babylonian Historical Texts Related to the Capture and Downfall of Babylon. Methuen & Co., 1924. pp. 100, 119. & R.P. Dougherty. Nabonidus and Belshazzar. Yale University Press, 1929. p. 107.

[435] W.F. Albright. The Biblical Period From Abraham to Ezra. p. 85.

[436] Ibid. pp. 84-85.

[437] Ibid. p. 86. See: Biblical Archaeology. V (1942). pp. 49ff. and Pritchard (Ed.). Ancient Near Eastern Texts Related to the Old Testament. p. 308.

[438] Randall Price. The Stones Cry Out. p. 235. Jane M. Cahill & David Tarler. "Excavations Directed by Yagael Shiloh at the City of David, 1978-1985." Hillel Geva (Ed.). Ancient Jerusalem Revealed. Israel Exploration Society, 1994. pp. 39-40.

[439] Ibid. Gabriel Barkay. "A Bulla of Ishmael, the King's Son." Bulletin of the American School of Oriental Research, 1993. 290-291. pp. 109-114.

[440] Ibid. See Hershel Shanks. "Jeremiah's Scribe and Confidant Speaks from a Hoard of Clay Bullae." Biblical Archaeology Review. September/October 1987. Vol. 13, No. 5. pp. 58-65.

[441] <www.baslibrary.org/biblical- archaeology-review/45/4/18> Biblical Archaeology Review. July-October 2019. Vol. 45, No. 4.

[442] Eilat Mazar. "Did I Find King David's Palace?" Biblical Archaeology Review. January/February 2006. <www.biblical archaeology.org/daily/biblical -topics-hebrew-bible-did-i-find-king-davids-palace/#note09>

[443] Ibid.
[444] Ibid. Randall Price Interview with Gabriel Barkay at Ketef Hinnom, Jerusalem. October 26, 1996.
[445] Kenneth A. Kitchen. On the Reliability of the Old Testament. p. 45.
[446] Bill Arnold & Bryan E. Beyer. Encountering the Old Testament. p. 435. Referencing John J. Collins. Daniel. IVP, 1969. p. 65.
[447] Ibid. Referencing: Joyce G. Baldwin. Daniel: An Introduction and Commentary. IVP, 1978. pp. 108-109.
[448] Ibid. Referencing: John C. Whitcomb. Darius the Mede: A Study in Historical Identification. Eerdmsns, 1959. & Donald J. Wiseman (Ed.). Notes on Some Problems in the Book of Daniel. Tyndale, 1963.
[449] Edwin Yamauchi. Composition and Corroboration on Classical and Biblical Studies. p. 31.
[450] Steven Anderson. "Darius the Mede: A Solution to His Identity." <truthonlybible.com/2016/01/08/darius-the-mede-a-solution-to-his-identity/>
[451] Ibid.
[452] Ibid.
[453] Ibid.
[454] W.F. Albright. The Biblical Period From Abraham to Ezra. p. 87. See: R. de Vaux. Review Biblique, 1937. pp. 29-57. & Eduard Meyer, H.H. Schaeder & E.J. Bickerman. Journal of Biblical Literature. (1946). LXV. pp. 249ff.
[455] J. Kenneth Eakins & Jack P. Lewis. "Archaeology and Biblical Study." p. 91.
[456] Randall Price. The Stones Cry Out. pp. 250-252.
[457] Ibid. pp. 251-252.
[458] Ibid. pp. 59-61. See: George G. Cameron. "Darius Carved History on Ageless Rock." National Geographic. December 1950. Vol. 96, No. 6. pp. 825-844.
[459] Ibid.
[460] Jack P. Lewis. Archaeological Backgrounds to Bible People. p. 125. Citing: A.T. Olmstead. History of the Persian Empire. University of Chicago Press, 1948. p. 227.
[461] Ibid. pp. 125-126. Referencing: J.B. Pritchard. Ancient Near Eastern Texts Related to the Old Testament. No. 463. & Olmstead. History of the Persian Empire. p. 285.
[462] Ibid. p. 130. Referring to Amherst Tablet #258 found at Borsippa. Now known as Birs Nimrud. It is 11 miles southwest of Babylon in Iraq.
[463] Ibid. A. Ungnad. "Kelienschriftliche Beitrage zum Buch Ezra und Ester." ZAW LVIII (1940/1941) 240-244, LIX (1942/1943) 219.
[464] Ibid. p. 128.
[465] Ibid. p. 135. Ungnad, Ibid. Also: A.T. Olmstead. "Tattenai, Governor of 'Across the River.'" Journal of Near Eastern Studies III (1944), 46.
[466] James L. Kelso. "The Archaeology of the Bible." p. 1198.
[467] Ibid. p. 90. See John Bright. A History of Israel. pp. 375-386. & Yehezkel Kaufmann. Jubilee Volume. (1960). pp. 70-87.

468 Ibid. Elephantine was a large island in the midst of the Nile River in Egypt where a colony of Jews had been established.

469 Edwin Yamauchi. Composition and Corroboration on Classical and Biblical Studies. pp. 24-25.

470 W.F. Albright. The Biblical Period From Abraham to Ezra. p. 87. See: The Murashu Archives for examples. One such site is: <cojs.org/the_murashu_archive_late_5th_century_bce/>

471 J. Kenneth Eakins & Jack P. Lewis. "Archaeology and Biblical Study." p. 91.

472 W.F. Albright. Archaeology and the Religion of Israel. John Hopkins Press, 1942. p. 176.

473 Bill Arnold & Bryan E. Beyer. Encountering the Old Testament. p. 435.

General Index

A

Aaron, Aaronic, 121, 128
Abaqa, 80
Abimelech, 72
Abraham, Abram, 16, 18, 22, 42, 51, 58, 62, 72, 74, 75, 77, 78, 79, 90, 96, 97, 98, 99, 101, 102, 103, 105, 106
accountability, 16
accuracy, accurate, 5, 8, 13, 23, 29, 34, 35, 36, 50, 58, 66, 70, 71, 72, 77, 79, 80, 82, 83, 87, 90, 91, 94, 95, 96, 98, 103, 108, 135, 138, 140, 144
Adad-nirari, 131
Adah, 62
Adam, 60
Ahab, 90, 125, 129, 130, 134
Ahaziahu, 125
Ahuramazda, 146
Akkadian, 48, 57, 77, 112
Albright, W.F., 50, 51, 71, 95, 100, 122, 147
Aleppo Codex, 28
Allegro, John, 33
Alliance, 74
alphabetical writing, 19
Amarna, 90, 126
Amorite, 77
Amraphel, 77
anachronisms, 39, 40
animism, 44, 46
annals, 129, 131, 137
antediluvian, 99
Anthropologist, anthropology, 44, 55, 111
Antiochus, 30
anti-supernatural, 53, 59, 73, 74, 95
apocrypha, apocryphal, 112, 139, 147
apostasy, 111, 128, 131
Aqabah, 127
Arab, Arabia, 94, 96, 102, 141
Aram, 129, 130
Aramaic, 11, 24, 25, 28, 29, 31, 32, 47, 81, 125, 131, 140, 147
Aramean, 25
Archaeologist, 23, 50, 75, 81, 91, 95, 105, 113, 125, 127, 143
Archer, Gleason, 26, 35, 69
argument, 5, 18, 19, 20, 21, 22, 42, 48, 50, 54, 55, 63, 69, 83, 113
Arioch, 77
Aristotle, 27

183

Biblia Hebraica Stuttgartensia, 35
Biblical criticism, 14, 18, 51, 56, 149
Bibliographic, 3, 25, 26, 65
birthright, 103
Bliss, F.J., 86
Bowman, Raymond, 95
British Museum, 137, 138
Bronze Age, 123
Bryant, Dewayne, 93, 120
bulla, 142, 143
Burrows, Miller, 95

C

Caesar's Gallic Wars, 26
Cairo, 31
camels, 102
Canaan, Canaanite, 23, 57, 61, 62, 74, 77, 81, 105, 111, 113, 115, 116, 117, 118, 119, 120, 121, 123, 124, 126, 129
Canon, canonical, 11, 12
carbon-14 dating, 36
Carchemish, 138
Catullus, 27
caves, 32, 35, 38
charnel houses, 105
Chedorlaomer, 77
Chesterton, G.K., 84
Chinese, 70
Chronicles, 1, 2 (O.T. Books), 12, 22, 59, 64, 80, 124, 129, 131, 132, 134, 137, 138
Cilicia, 89
clarifying, 89
Codex, 28
coherence, 40, 41
Colson, Chuck, 84
conclusion, 8, 10, 27, 46, 69, 148, 182
confirms, conformation, 6, 125, 131
conquest, 63, 77, 113, 115, 116, 119, 122, 123, 126, 131, 132, 133, 135, 137, 138, 140, 141, 149
consistency, 7, 26, 40, 105
consonants, 13, 20
context, 8, 35, 40, 52, 63, 90, 91
contracts (Near Eastern), 72
contradictions, 5, 6, 39, 40, 50, 53, 59, 68, 122
conventional, 17
conviction, 9
copper mines, 80
corroboration, corroborating, 40, 71, 79, 115, 116, 120
covenant, 72, 103
create, created, 16, 22, 37, 39, 43, 50, 52, 54, 55, 56, 60, 61, 63, 68, 87, 90, 97, 98, 99, 128

F

187

189

M

Q

R

192

S

T

translations, 26, 28, 29, 30, 34, 37, 89, 91, 108
transmission, transmitted, 11, 27, 29, 34, 35, 65, 107
Turkey, 74, 78, 89, 100, 101
Tyre, Tyre's, 129, 139, 140

U

Ugalet, 78
Ugarit, 89
Ugaritic, 57, 89
unique, uniqueness, 20, 21, 34, 66, 94, 98, 114, 121, 148, 181
unity, 7, 41, 49
unreliable, 5, 13, 25, 35, 46, 53, 63, 73, 94, 99
Ur, 74, 97, 100

V

valid, 15, 18, 27, 39, 40, 41, 43, 55, 57, 77, 79, 91, 100
validate, invalidate, 34, 42, 51, 69, 111, 119
variants, variations, 26, 35, 36, 38, 49, 50, 56, 98, 109
vassal treaties, 136
verify, verifiable, 6, 9, 18, 58, 65, 82, 93, 94, 132
versions, 37, 38, 70, 109, 182

W

Waitke, Bruce, 36, 37
Wellhausen, Julius, 43
Wilson, Edmund, 33
Wilson, Robert Dick, 6, 9, 15, 25, 69, 97, 149
Wiseman, Donald J., 91, 138
Wood, Bryant, 105, 113, 127
Wooley, Sir Charles Leonard, 8
worldview, 73, 74, 99, 115
Wouk, Herman, 51, 149

X

Xenophon, 144
Xerxes, 145, 146

Y

Yahweh, 29, 41, 72, 108, 111, 114, 118, 128, 133, 143
Yamauchi, Edwin, 56, 57, 92
Yehuchal, 143
Yeno'am, Yenoam, 119

Z

Select Bibliography

Arnold, Bill T. & Bryan E. Beyer. Encountering the Old Testament. Baker Books, 1999.

Brotzman, Ellis. Old Testament Textual Criticism. Baker Books, 1994.

Bryant, Dewayne. "The Bible's Buried Secrets." Reason & Revelation. August 2009. Vol. 29, No. 8. pp. 1-5, 8-10.

Eakins, J. Kenneth & Jack Lewis. "Archaeology and Biblical Study." Trent C. Butler. (Ed.). Holman Bible Dictionary. 1991. pp. 83-93.

Kaiser, Walter C. Jr. The Old Testament Documents: Are they Reliable & Relevant? IVP, 2001.

Kennedy, D. James. What If The Bible Had Never Been Written? Thomas Nelson, 1998.

Kitchen, Kenneth. On the Reliability of the Old Testament. Eerdman's Publishing Co., 2003.

Lightfoot, Neil R. How We Got the Bible. Baker Books, 3rd ed., 2003.

McDowell, Josh. New Evidence That Demands A Verdict. Thomas Nelson, 1999.

Massod, Steven. The Bible and the Qu'ran: A Question of Integrity. Paternoster Publishing, 2001.

Nelson, Ethel R. & Richard E. Broadberry. Genesis and the Mystery Confucius Couldn't Solve. Concordia Publishing House, 1994.

Price, Randall. The Stones Cry Out. Harvest House, 1997.

Walton, John, et al. The IVP Bible Background Commentary: Old Testament. IVP, 2000.

Wilson, Robert Dick. A Scientific Investigation of the Old Testament. Moody Press, 1959.

Wood, Bryan J. "Did the Israelites Conquer Jericho? A New Look at the Archaeological Evidence." Shanks, Hershall (Ed.). Biblical Archaeology Review. March/April 1990. Vol. XVI, No. 2. pp. 44-59.

Wood, Bryan. "Dating Jericho's Destruction: Bienkowski is Wrong on All Counts." Shanks, Hershall (Ed.). Biblical Archaeology Review. September/October 1990. Vol. XVI, No. 5. pp. 45-47, 49, 68-69.

Yurco, Frank J. "3,200-Year-Old Picture of Israelites Found in Egypt." Shanks, Hershall (Ed.). Biblical Archaeology Review. September/October 1990. Vol. XVI, No. 2. pp. 20-38.

Other Books by Dr. Gerald Charles Tilley

The Origin of Religion. The secular explanations as to the Origin of religion are rejected as lacking evidence and contradicting the evidence available.

The Uniqueness of the Christian Faith. (4th Edition). Professor Tilley explains more than a dozen ways historic, biblical Christianity is unique and does not fit in the same category as the world religions.

The Absurdity of Atheism. (2nd Edition). This book shows that science, history, and human reason prove atheism to be absurd. Some of the irrational and dishonest methods and attempts to justify atheism are exposed.

The Origin of the Mormon Religion. The historical background of the early 1800's, the lives of Joseph Smith and his family as well as the early history of the religion itself prove Mormonism (the LDS Church) to be anti-Christian. This refutes current claims to be a Christian Church.

The Two Faces of Islam. In most of the world, Islam is known as a violent religion that persecutes and kills opponents. In the West, Muslim advocates claim Islam is a religion of peace and reconciliation. The Quran presents both versions of Islam. One of these predominates throughout its history.

Defending the Christian Faith. (2nd Edition). This book consists of about a dozen apologetics essays that seek to show the authenticity, historicity, and reliability of the biblical scriptures and that the Christian Faith is true.

Colossians: The Supremacy & Sufficiency of Christ. This is a basic Greek word study and commentary on the Apostle Paul's letter to the Colossian Church.

Is Jesus Christ Alive? This brand-new book presents evidence including evidence outside of the Bible that Jesus rose from the dead. It also refutes theories devised to avoid the evidence and conclusion of the resurrection.

The Protestant Reformations of the 16th Century. This book presents many of the participants in the Lutheran, Calvinist and Anabaptist Reformations.

Made in the USA
Columbia, SC
10 November 2024

45934928R00109